MULE DEER

HUNTING TODAY'S
TROPHIES

Pursuing the Gray Ghost

BY JIM VAN NORMAN & TOM CARPENTER

Published by

 **krause**
publications

700 E. State Street • Iola, WI 54990-0001
Telephone: 715/445-2214

Please call or write for our free catalog.
Our toll-free number to place an order or obtain a free catalog is 800-258-0929
or please use our regular business telephone 715-445-2214
for editorial comment and further information.

Library of Congress Catalog Number: 90-60576
ISBN: 0-87341-563-9

Printed in the United States of America

Contents

About the Authors

Jim Van Norman

Jim Van Norman was born and raised in Wyoming. Since he was big enough to follow his dad hunting he has paid special attention to mule deer. Van Norman took his first mule deer buck at 11, as you'll read, and has been an increasingly hopeless addict ever since.

As an author and photographer, Van Norman's articles and photos have appeared in national magazines and books. The majority of mule deer photos in this book are his. He hopes to further his endeavors in these areas. He is also the author of a booklet called *30 Years Chasin' Mule Deer, Some of My Best Thinkin'*, a field guide, so to speak, to this fireplace volume on hunting trophy mule deer.

Jim and his wife Perri manage a large cattle ranch in northcentral Wyoming and have the great privilege of observing mule deer 365 days a year. Jim, along with Perri's hard work and efforts in fine cuisine, also operates a successful outfitting business on the ranch for mule deer, antelope and elk.

Jim's company, Northfork Outfitters, has enjoyed the insights and hunting company of the legendary M.R. James, Founder/Editor in Chief of *Bowhunter Magazine*, and the good fortune of being featured a few times in the magazine. He has also enjoyed the expertise in the bow-hunting business world and hunting company of *Bowhunter Magazine's* Associate Publisher/Advertising Director, Fred Wallace.

Jim Van Norman

Mule deer and antelope hunts with Northfork Outfitters have also been featured on *The American Archer* TV program, hosted by archery great Tom Nelson of Anderson Archery, Grandledge, Michigan.

Van Norman's hunting and guiding experience has spanned 33 years. He has been fortunate enough to collect many of his own trophies with bow and rifle. Those species include mule deer, Kodiak Island brown bear, white-tailed deer, black bear, elk, pronghorn antelope, mountain lion, bighorn sheep and caribou. He also participates yearly in hunting upland and migratory game birds, fly fishing and is an avid varmint hunter.

Jim spends the majority of his life outdoors. He enjoys sharing his experiences and providing others with great outdoor experiences — especially young, up-and-coming outdoor enthusiasts.

Tom Carpenter

Tom Carpenter is a born-and-bred Midwesterner raised with big game hunting in his blood and a love for everything about the outdoors, particularly hunting and fishing. But he is a Westerner at heart, spending much time each year in the great American West. There he has developed a special love for mule deer and mule deer hunting. Carpenter is also duly addicted to whitetails, pronghorns, grouse of all kinds, trout, bird watching (the list goes on), and writing about it all.

Carpenter's other books include works on whitetails, pronghorns and upland birds. His magazine articles on the outdoors have been published in national magazines.

Tom lives in Minnesota with his wife Julie and their brood of three sons: Jeremiah, Ethan and Noah.

Tom Carpenter.

Acknowledgments

Loving mule deer, and the prairies and peaks they call home, is a wonderful addiction. But to create a book as complete and far-ranging as this, even experienced mule deer fanatics like us need help and insight. Therefore, we acknowledge the following individuals for their time, energy and contributions:

Chuck Carpenter of Wellsville, Utah, for pulling together the basis of the chapter "The Work Begins." John Spaulding and Steve Warner for their hunting companionship, past and present, as well as insight during this writing. Ron Bahls of Hamburg, Minnesota, for artwork. Daren Cornforth of Utah State University and Dick Whittier of the Meat Lab at USU, for their expertise regarding field and meat care. Jim Campbell, taxidermist from Wellsville, Utah, for his advice on the caping information. And the following individuals for their time and thoughts in outlining their states' mule deer hunting opportunities: Karl Menzel, Nebraska Game and Parks Commission; Jay Lawson, Wyoming Game and Fish Department; Brad Frano, Colorado Division of Wildlife; Rolf Johnson, Washington Department of Fish & Wildlife; Lonn Kuck, Idaho Fish & Game Department; Mike Welch, Utah Division of Wildlife Resources; Bob Mathews, Kansas Department of Wildlife and Parks; Russ Mohr, California Department of Fish & Game; Ray Lee, Arizona Game & Fish Department; Glenn Erickson, Montana Department of Fish, Wildlife and Parks; Tom Keegan, Oregon Department of Fish & Wildlife; Darryl Weybright, New Mexico Department of Fish & Game; Mike Hobson, Texas Parks & Wildlife Department; Mary Ann Holliday and Mike Hess, Nevada Division of Wildlife; Jerry Schaw, Oklahoma Department of Wildlife Conservation; Bill Jensen, North Dakota Game & Fish Department; Ken Moum, South Dakota Department of Game, Fish and Parks.

Dedication

To my wife Perri who understands my unquenchable thirst for the outdoors and hunting, and endures my passion for exposing hidden mule deer.

To my father, God rest his soul, for taking the time from his busy schedule to teach me the ways of hunting and the outdoors.

For my mother who encouraged me to always pursue, in life, what you have the greatest passion for.

And to Raymond Allemand, Perri's father, who gave us the grand opportunity for a continued lifestyle in the outdoors.

Jim Van Norman

To Julie, my first and only love, for being there through every hunting season and still loving me at the end of each one.

And to Jeremiah, Ethan and Noah, that they too may one day see and experience the wonders of the West and its mule deer.

Tom Carpenter

Prologue

Mule Deer Firsts

What better way to start a hunting book than with a couple of good stories? It will let you get a little acquainted with us, the co-authors, and maybe even explain a little bit about why we love mule deer – and hunting them – so much. Then we'll dive headlong into the nitty-gritty of hunting today's trophy mule deer bucks.

Mule Deer Savvy

I was born and bred in Wyoming, and still make my home there. Probably always will. My grammar is not the greatest and my vocabulary is limited to my "out in the sticks" upbringing, so I deliver the knowledge in this book as if you were crawling through the brush alongside me. Tell you like I'd tell you, if you were here, hunting right along with me. The editors and I (even Tom and I!) have "butted heads" a little along those lines. But I think we have worked together well to make the book both "grammatically informative," yet interesting and fun!

Before we delve into the technical aspects of this writing though, I'd like to share with you a story that first made me realize mule deer bucks are able to apply whatever level of intelligence is necessary for survival. In sharing this with you I hope to set the stage in your quest for more knowledge and prepare you for what to expect once you've dared engage the world of trophy mule deer. (God save your schoolwork, jobs and marriages!)

It was 1965, the first year I was allowed to carry a rifle while deer hunting. I was 11 years old. Although not legal, my father allowed I could take his deer. I had been on several deer hunts with Dad in previous years and took note of many techniques. However, when Dad said, in his gruff and tough manner, "I just saw five big bucks go up that draw there and none of 'em came out— go and get one!", I swallowed hard.

I took a few steps in that direction, then turned to ask a question. But the look I received answered everything. I had hounded him several years for this opportunity and here it was. I had learned to swim in a similar manner and survived. Although not the way we teach kids these days, it was his way. So, I began stalking up the draw.

Jim's love of mule deer started early.

My rifle was a .30-30 carbine with open sights. I put seven rounds in the magazine and one in the barrel (with the hammer in the safety position) for a total of eight. Plus I had five extra rounds in my pocket. I guess I thought I would be ready for anything that moved, ran or charged!

At that age, the terrain loomed huge ahead of me. The hills that surrounded the draw were mountains, the sagebrush looked like trees and the side walls of the washouts I skirted resembled cliffs of a massive gorge. The acres of countryside around me faded and there lay ahead only an enchanted canyon with five monsters in hiding. Scared? Not me! Just a little excited. Ya right!

As I eased along I tried to remember what to look for– a horn, a white face, an ear. I knew they would be bedded in the shade and remembered dad saying once that big bucks seldom lay in the main draw but instead generally lay in the little side draws that branched from a main draw. Around the next corner was one of those side draws! It was short and steep, with tall sagebrush and the left side, facing north, had tons of shade. I looked down at my thumb, making sure it was positioned on the hammer of my rifle. Simultaneously, a rabbit jumped from beneath my feet and I about "fouled my britches!" Upon regaining semi-composure, I searched the shade with my naked eye but saw nothing.

Slowly walking to the end of the wash I looked in every hiding spot I could think of, but there was nothing. I turned around to see where I had been and the shady slope exploded! Not thirty yards away, sprang five big monarch bucks with antlers to the sky! They had let me walk right by them!

The first three shots, I think I bunch shot 'em. The next four, I did try to concentrate on one buck, but they all bounded up and over the steep face as if I wasn't even there. When the smoke cleared, I hadn't scratched a hair! Shaking like a leaf, I sat on a rock and could not believe what had just happened. Dad was gonna' be pissed!

I began reloading my rifle and was looking up to recount the event, when something caught my eye. There, a short 20 yards away, was an antler sticking out of the sagebrush, by a small cut bank. Hooked to that antler was the stark white face of a buck, ears laid back, hiding for all he was worth. I couldn't believe my eyes. There were six bucks, not five! I looked away immediately to make the deer think I hadn't see him. Then, I eased the hammer back, raised up and shot him where he lay. Heck, I could have hit him with a stick. I don't even remember aiming! The buck rolled down the hill a little way then lay still. My knees were shaking so much I could hardly walk up to him.

I got one! A darn nice five-by-four. While I was busy "puffing up" and admiring the buck, Dad came out of nowhere. I think he had followed me and watched the whole thing but, he never said so. He shook my hand and congratulated me. Although he also scolded me lightly for shooting so much and not picking one buck and one spot on that buck while shooting, I could tell he was still proud. After looking at the buck's teeth or lack of same, Dad determined him to be quite old. A buck

that was probably a lot bigger at one time in his life and had seen many-a hunting season.

Can you believe that buck would lay there all that time while a barrage of gunfire hailed over his head and rang like thunder in that little basin? I guarantee that buck had used this tactic several times before and survived. Although I've seen many-a trick, I haven't seen anything quite like it since. But that doesn't mean it hasn't happened to me again. I'm sure many-a trophy buck has slipped away unnoticed while laughing at old Jim Van Norman.

From that magical day forward, a hunting spell was cast that I have never been able to shake. So, I've given trophy mule deer bucks the respect they deserve and have spent as much time as possible in the field observing them. As you read this book and during your subsequent trips to the field, I hope you're able to develop a special appreciation for these sorcerers of detection and wit, as well as experience the magic in each of their pristine domains.

JVN

Another Mule Deer "First"

Unlike Jim, I was not born into a world with mule deer, but rather discovered them when I was in my twenties. Every autumn since has found me back in mule deer country, usually in more than one state, from Arizona on up through Colorado, Wyoming, Utah, Idaho and Montana. But chief among my mule deer memories are those of my first muley buck and the Idaho mountain I found him on.

When you're raised hunting whitetails, nothing can prepare you for the sight of a steel-gray deer pogo-sticking up an unbelievable slope, or those huge mule deer ears, or even the size of some forkhorns' racks. That's the whole new experience I found as that hunt started.

My brother Chuck (a naturalized Utahan), Daren Cornforth (a dedicated big-muley addict) and I would work our way out from our camp, a simple tent in a wind-protected, maple brush draw, each November day. It was the tail end of Idaho's season, and we were hoping to find some bucks hanging around the does.

One morning we climbed the right drainage, and seemed to get to the right elevation at the right time. Deer were moving, and the Westerners had to restrain me from shooting at a couple of big forkhorns that were out and about. The November sun, which had been peeking over the ridges to the east when we set out from the sage at the base of this mountain, was now warming our backs.

As we glassed a couple does in a canyon bottom, a much bigger and darker deer appeared out of the brush. The shot was long and the angle steep, but this was a good buck and a good opportunity as he stood in a small clearing, seeming to soak up the first rays of sun to hit the canyon bottom. Patient glassing and using the thermal air currents (rising as the sun warmed the canyon sides and bottoms) to our advantage had paid off.

I scrambled into the sling and a sitting position, touched off a shot, then worked the bolt and shot again. The echoes bounced back and forth on the steep, brushy canyon walls. But the buck only took one step; he wasn't going to panic until he knew where the danger was coming from. A quick whisper from one of my partners reminded me that though the shot was long, the angle was steep and I probably wouldn't need to hold high.

The buck leaped at my last shot. We heard some crunching and crashing in the brush. Then everything was still. It took 45 minutes to work our way down the slope, through brush and across two icy-cold mountain streams to where the four-by-four buck had come to rest.

He was gray and big and beautiful to me. His antlers were chocolate brown from rubbing the fir trees and maple brush. I ran my hands through his thick, sage-scented coat before we snapped a few pictures, and then set to work dressing him out in the quiet, secluded canyon of the southern Idaho mountain.

I have been addicted to mule deer ever since. They are a challenge and a joy to hunt, and a big part of that joy is the magnificent mountain, foothill, sagebrush, prairie, badlands and desert country that the deer draw me to.

TJC

Tom and brother Chuck with an Idaho buck.

10

Chapter 1

Introduction

Hide and Seek

Ever notice that human nature, all through life, provokes us to hide and observe, or seek out the hidden? Whether a genetic characteristic or a behavioral quirk, it's present in all of us at some level. It is just plain fascinating to find the hidden things that, though obvious, were totally invisible until we knew how and where to look for them. This is an alluring element of all hunting. And, as hunters, we all seem to thrive on this and other elements such as secrecy, adrenaline, surprise and success.

Hunting today's trophy mule deer provides these experiences against the backdrop of the wild and wide-open spaces of the great American West.

Trophy mule deer present a hide-and-seek contest of epic proportions in every habitat type they occupy – becoming true gray ghosts of each landscape, from the peaks to the prairies. Mule deer hide in some of the most pristine and lonely landscapes on earth. They can also nearly disappear in some of the most barren ones. Each of these Western panoramas offers a beauty and romance all its own. True mule deer fanatics are willing to go from cactus deserts to sagebrush prairies; from high plains badlands and canyon country to timbered alpine mountainsides; to oxygen-starved peaks in search of a trophy.

No matter the result of your mule deer quest, just seeing and enjoying mule deer country will make any trip worthwhile.

You can generally observe mule deer often in the field, thanks to the lack of heavy cover (in most cases) in mule deer habitat, and the docile attitude of most does, fawns and younger, inexperienced bucks. This, in itself, makes mule deer hunting enjoyable. People who have not hunted mule deer are often amazed at the number of deer they get to see. It's the trophy bucks, the big gray ghosts, that often elude detection. But they are out there.

Rest assured. If you're in a decent area and you hunt using the strategies, tactics and tips in this book, you'll find big mule deer. You'll find the best deer your area has to offer.

Defining "Trophy"

Now the phrase "trophy mule deer" conjures up images of magazine-cover bucks sporting wide, deep-forked, heavy racks against a backdrop of golden aspens and dark green pockets of pines. The buck is Boone and Crockett material and the landscape is classic.

But for many of today's mule deer hunters, be you a resident of a mule deer state or a visitor from any other area of the country, "trophy" usually means a mature buck for the area being hunted. That deer must, of course, be taken under the rules of fair chase. As far as we are concerned though, a trophy mule deer is always in the eyes of the beholder who has just harvested it. And that's as it should be.

So, this trophy could be a four-by-four buck with a 20-inch spread from a heavily-hunted area in Utah or Colorado. That's a mature buck for the area being hunted. A forkhorn from any state could be considered a trophy for a young or first-time mule deer hunter. An adult doe taken on a stalk by a Montana longbow hunter is just as much a trophy as a gray-muzzled, wide-racked Wyoming ridge runner for a dyed-in-the-wool mule deer addict who might only pull the trigger on a "big-enough" buck once every three seasons. No matter what your definition, any mule deer you decide to try to harvest is a trophy, and the experience is truly one to be remembered. But make no mistake,

Here are two nice typical muley bucks. These are fine, mature deer.

the biggest and most experienced bucks in any given area are a mindset apart from the area's average mule deer. Most of our strategies and techniques, when applied consistently, are designed to yield more quality opportunities at these bigger, more experienced bucks. Once you've learned to apply these tactics, you'll find that all your trophy mule deer will come a bit more easily whether you are hunting with a bow, muzzleloader or rifle.

Counting Points

Throughout this book, we'll use "Western count" when describing mule deer bucks, and count all the points on one antler. We use the Wyoming definition of "point", which is any tine you can hang a ring on. For instance, the phrase "four-

A nice 5x5 buck. Those are exceptionally-long brow tines for a mule deer.

by-four" (4x4) used previously indicates a deer with four points on each antler. That buck might also be called a "four-pointer" or "four-point" depending on the locale. An Eastern, Southern or Midwestern whitetail hunter would call this buck an eight-pointer.

Yet even across mule deer range, hunters' use of "Western count" differs. In some areas, brow tines are not traditionally counted. This means your basic four-by-four could actually have five points on each antler, but the brow tines wouldn't be counted.

You should also know that in some places, notably Utah, spread is king. A buck may be a true six-by-five, but you wouldn't know it unless you saw a picture of it because the hunter will just say, "I got a 28-inch buck." There seems to be something magical about spread, especially when it's close to the 30-inch mark. When you're talking spread though, be sure to define whether you're discussing inside measurement or the widest (outside) measurement; either way, something like that 28-inch spread is impressive. But if you're into record books, take a look at Boone and Crockett or Pope and Young length of beam, mass and points will carry you much farther than spread; you only get one spread measurement, and that could even count against you.

Focusing on Mature Bucks

Big, mature mule deer – the ones many hunters want to focus on – are one of the most sought-after trophies in modern times. Magnificent antlers and limited mule deer distribution contributes to this fact, as does the increasing intelligence of today's mule deer. An older muley buck may well be North America's most challenging big-game animal.

With increased "people pressure" ranging from human encroachment into their habitat to relatively heavy hunting pressure, today's muley bucks become more elusive at an earlier age. We believe a mature mule deer buck is as challenging to hunt and bag as any big whitetail. In fact, mule deer could well be a tougher challenge, if they occupied the same habitat as their white-tailed relatives.

Why? Because whitetails can often be patterned and mule deer generally cannot. Whitetails, despite all their secrecy and nocturnal tendencies, can often be expected along certain trails or at certain locations. Not so with mule deer bucks. Because of their tendency for random roaming (browsing with no particular direction in mind), the large size of their home range and the sensitivity of their acute instincts, harvesting trophy mule deer in any type of heavy cover could be, and in some areas has proven to be, more difficult than harvesting a mature white-tailed buck.

Tomorrow's mature bucks.

Even without heavy cover, today's mule deer have adopted many of the tricks and survival strategies commonly attributed only to the master whitetail. To add to the challenge, mule deer have a lot more range in which to apply these strategies, and are almost always more spread out in their habitat.

Big, experienced mule deer bucks do not get big by just being extremely lucky. Although they sometimes seem to lead charmed lives, these bucks acquire the knowledge to survive through many successful escapes, including motionless "nerves-of-steel" hiding and completely avoiding any potential danger. Proof of the latter is a mature buck's tendency to go to the most Godforsaken, out-of-the-way habitat available upon the first hint of hunting pressure. He may well be living there before the guns go off anyway. His wonderful nose, incredible ears, spectacular eyesight and strategic bedding habits allow a buck mule deer to assess situations early on and escape detection. He creates his own luck to grow big and old.

With danger approaching, mule deer are more apt to get up and leave the area at a walk, long before the problem is threatening. But if the danger is not noticed until it is relatively close, today's mule deer bucks will hide with even more patience and daring than their white-tailed cousins. They will often let the danger pass sometimes within a few feet, then sneak away after "it" is gone. Bolting is a last resort. However, if the deer thinks you have seen him he will break the front and back doors down, possibly running you over, on his way out!

The Cornerstone to Success

Understanding the above characteristics is the key to successful mule deer hunting. Finding mule deer, long before they find you, is the cornerstone to being a successful trophy mule deer hunter. Actually, the concept is the cornerstone to being a great hunter, period. But of everything covered in this book, this skill (ac-

tually a combination of several techniques) is the one to be mastered. Learning to spot mule deer before they spot you is a lot more difficult than it sounds. The trick is to find every single deer in a given drainage, without them being aware of your presence. That's tougher than you might think.

Without developing this cornerstone skill, you will not have the opportunity to apply the other knowledge found in this book. Those bigger, smarter bucks will simply leave the area at a walk, or hide and let you pass, then slip away after you are gone ... and they will laugh at you as they go.

We will spend a great deal of time on this subject and support the facts with graphics, photographs and text. If you hunt mule deer regularly, you're sure to pick up some new insights here. If you are an occasional or first-time mule deer hunter, review this particular information religiously.

Supporting the Key Skill

We also dedicate an entire chapter to full-color photos of hidden mule deer, allowing you to apply the knowledge and test your skill. The deer in these pictures are totally wild muleys. See how hard it is to spot each one, and how easy it is to look past members of a mule deer group or a single buck on the fringe.

Of course, the foundation of this book presents spotting mule deer as the cornerstone to success. But there still has to be rhyme and reason to the way you go about hunting muleys, no matter what type of habitat you're hunting or what time of the season you're doing it. So we'll show you: where to look to find mule deer; how to get around the countryside without being noticed; how to stalk muleys successfully once you find them; and more. Everything is outlined step-by-step. We'll also talk about field care essentials for mule deer country, selecting a state to hunt in and planning your hunt.

More than 40 years of combined experience hunting mule deer with rifles, muzzleloaders, bows and cameras, guiding hunters, and the blessing of living with mule deer 365 days a year contributes to this work. We hope you enjoy reading it as much as we enjoyed putting it together. We also hope you will pick up some useful skills that will bring you many successful seasons chasin' mule deer.

To start, just thumb through the book and take a look at the many pictures and diagrams provided. Get a feel for mule deer and start the mental process of defining where to look and what to look for. Then hunker down and let the pages take you right out to mule deer country, in search of the gray ghosts of peaks and prairies.

Chapter 2
The Magnificent Mule Deer

A Different Kind of Deer

"As I gazed through my binoculars I did a double-take on the back line of some critter just over a little rise and out about 200 yards. The body was fairly blocky so I concluded it to be a buck of some sort. But when he lifted his head above the rise my mouth went agape! There was no doubt I was looking at one of the biggest set of antlers I'd ever seen on a deer! He was big and gray and so heavy ... muscles like I'd never seen before on any buck. Here, all rolled into one, were grand antlers, sheer power and dignified grace ... a mule deer."

That's an actual account from a dyed-in-the-wool whitetail hunter sharing his first encounter with a big mule deer buck. That hunter, like thousands of other traditional whitetail hunters who make treks west to pursue mule deer, has been hooked on mule deer ever since. Many Westerners who live and hunt in mule deer country are equally addicted.

In addition to our need to hunt and to get out in the wide open spaces of the West, there's one common bond that all mule deer hunters share: a love of mule deer. Part of this stems from being in the country muleys inhabit. The other part comes from knowing the deer. Mule deer are creatures of the West, and have evolved their own unique lifestyle and survival strategies. Knowing the deer will also make you a better hunter.

So this book provides a basic description of mule deer. Now, there are some very good technical books on mule deer. They are large, very complete and very informative; some are listed in the appendix. But this is a hunting book. There's not room to cover every fascinating aspect of mule deer biology and behavior. We'd never get any hunting strategies outlined! So there's no technical or biological razzle-dazzle here, just real, first-hand information based on years of observing and hunting mule deer. By reading this book you will gain insights to help you appreciate muleys even more, and hunt them more effectively.

Your Basic Mule Deer

We recognize the fact that mule deer have subspecies such as the desert mule deer and the California mule deer. But in the end they're just mule deer. Most of us will end up hunting that basic mule deer – the Rocky Mountain variety – anyway. This is the deer you'll find from the eastern fringes of mule deer range (the central Dakotas down through Texas) westward through the mountain states to the crest of the Sierras, and from the range's northern extremes in Canada down through the mountains of the U.S. desert Southwest. In the end, they're just mule deer wherever you find them, and they're just great to know and hunt.

Body and Antlers

Most first-time mule deer hunters are in awe of mule deer bodies and antlers when first setting eyes on a mature mule deer buck. The whitetails these hunters usually see are just sleeker and more streamlined, with smaller, neat, symmetrical racks that don't grow nearly as high or wide. An adult mule deer's overall body length is approximately 6 1/2 feet, with a shoulder of about 3 to 3 1/2 feet. Mule deer bucks on the hoof can weigh from 125 pounds for an immature buck to a whopping 300 pounds on the hoof for a mature buck. Does range between 100 and 150 pounds.

Mule deer buck with antlers in velvet.

Real Numbers On Real Bucks

The largest buck I have ever weighed, and I haven't weighed them all, bottomed the scales out at 242 pounds field dressed. That's a lot of deer, probably 300 pounds on the hoof. It was shot near my home in central Wyoming. The average mature buck I see harvested, and I see quite a few in the course of a year, weighs 250 to 265 pounds on the hoof. That's definitely bigger than an average whitetail most anywhere.

JVN

Mule deer antlers are large and impressive compared to other deer species. Muley antlers also have a different configuration. Typical whitetail antlers have points that all protrude from one main beam. Mule deer antlers have another branch on the main beam, and points grow from both the main beam and the branch. The two main points that grow from the branch beam are the back tines, technically referred to as the G2 and G3 points. The G4 point is the major point that branches from the main beam. The main beam is just that, the major beam that all other points and branches stem from. The G1 is the brow tine. Refer to the Boone and Crockett score sheet in the appendix for further clarification.

Classic whitetail (left) and mule deer bucks.

Mule deer, like whitetails and most other deer species, shed their antlers and grow a new set each year. The new antlers grow all summer, and it's interesting that many bucks will keep their velvet until well into September, with some bucks not cleaning it off until the last week of that month. Bucks can shed their

This buck has just lost his antlers.

antlers as early as December and as late as March. But for the most part, late January into February seems to be when the majority of shedding takes place, at least in the central Wyoming country we're most familiar with.

Any mule deer buck will look good, the first time you see one. Even yearling forkhorns can have fairly impressive racks, compared to the average whitetail. The best advice? If you'd like a big rack, don't shoot the first mule deer you see, unless you have an educated coach telling you it really is a good one. Do some shopping first.

Coloration

Mule deer coloration varies from summer to winter just as with other deer species. Spring finds the mule deer in transition between a long winter coat of gray and a new, shorter coat of a light reddish brown color. Mule deer look rougher at this time of year than any other. As the bucks and does begin to get more green nourishment, the long hair of winter is

This rough-looking buck is going through his transition from summer to winter coat.

shed completely and the deer take on a reddish orange, almost copper, color. This coloration makes them stand out like a sore thumb, no matter what habitat they reside in. It's a great time to go out and glass for mule deer because you can usually locate them easily.

In August, muleys begin the transition to their fall and winter coat of gray. The start of the transition varies from year to year depending on the weather. On extremely wet years they seem to start graying up earlier than dry years. Mule deer are also hard to see when they are in the brown-to-gray transition period of August, when some archery seasons are open. The bucks' faces are also in transition to a stark white at this time, making their muzzles harder to pick out while glassing. Also, their rumps are not as white during the summer months as they are later in the year, and the black tips on their tails are not as prominent.

You will note considerable differences in mule deer coloration from area to area. Mule deer as well as other wildlife have an uncanny ability to evolve colors that benefit them in the particular habitat they have pioneered. A good place to take note of this coloration difference is in your local taxidermy shop. Compare capes of deer taken from the mountains versus deer from the high plains and desert country. The differences are quite noticeable and noteworthy. Deer from areas with more precipitation are generally much darker than those from drier, more arid areas.

Getting Around

Mule deer are fascinating for many reasons. But their most unusual characteristic may well be the pogo-sticking, stiff-legged, jumping they use while escaping danger. The scientists call this stotting and that's as good a word as any because this method of getting from here to there defies conventional description.

Muleys developed the stotting form of movement specifically for the purpose of elud-

---

Hybrids Don't Stott

Hybrid crosses between mule deer and whitetails (becoming more common in parts of the West where the species' ranges are overlapping) are generally born without the ability to stott. That fact, along with other poor instincts inherent in the cross, make the hybrid's chances for long-term survival slim. I have, however, seen reasonably mature bucks with mule deer bodies and whitetail antlers, so there must be some exceptions to the rule. Nevertheless, stotting is a very important asset in a mule deer's arsenal of survival skills.

JVN

---

ing predators. It is bred into a mule deer's genes because muleys that don't stott probably don't survive to make additional mule deer.

A mule deer can run as fast as a whitetail if it decides to, and if it has some flat ground to work on. But when startled or avoiding predators, a mule deer invariably chooses to stott. While stotting, a mule deer can bound straight up hills or cut banks, over tall brush or just about any obstacle within reason. The hopping motion of stotting also means the deer can change direction in an instant, making a pretty tough target for any predator including a human with a rifle. In addition, stotting helps the deer see what's up ahead as it bounds along.

Stotting is paramount for a mule deer's survival because of the sloped, uneven terrain they normally inhabit.

Ears, Eyes And Nose

Another prominent mule deer characteristic, the one from which the muley's name originates, is the large ears. They're almost mule-like in their size and shape. Simply put, that tremendous ear surface area, catching sounds of all kinds, means mule deer have a wonderfully keen sense of hearing. And the deer pay extreme attention to their hearing; it is one of their main defenses. When having heard something disturbing, even at great distances, mule deer (especially older bucks) will quietly leave the area long before potential danger has a chance to show up. Mule deer trust their ears.

Mule deer eyesight is also excellent. They possess a special ability to detect movement like no other critter of the prairies, badlands, hills and mountains, save for maybe the bug-eyed pronghorn. But a mule deer's overall ability to spot danger by sight is, in our estimation, comparable to that of the pronghorn. And that's saying a lot! And a muley's peripheral vision is, to say the least, extreme.

In addition, a mule deer's scent detection abilities are acute – no small task in the arid country they usually inhabit. There's just no getting around the fact that a mule deer can smell you from a very long distance if the wind is just right. A muley's nose is a third great defense for locating danger. To be successful hunting mule deer in any situation, you have to always evaluate the wind properly, no question about it and no exceptions. We'll discuss this in detail in some of the chapters to come.

When bedding in an ideal situation, a mule deer will position itself in a place where it has a panoramic view in front, is well-hidden, and the wind is at his or her back. This way they can see on-coming problems, smell any problems from behind and hear warnings of any danger from around the compass.

Nobody has asked a mule deer, but if you had to rank these senses in order of importance, sight is probably their number one defense preference, followed by their ears and then their nose. But make no mistake. Neither is better than the other. Danger noticed by any one of them can bust the best of hunters!

Communication

Mule deer communicate vocally, but probably not quite as aggressively as the whitetail. Mule deer of both sexes do "talk" back and forth as they feed along in a group. Does seem to talk the most, as they communicate to their fawns regularly.

During the rut you will note more vocalization than normal. At this time there is also a good deal of "posturing" between the bucks as they attempt to display dominance and figure out who's the big guy on the block. Much of this communication is not vocal, but behavioral.

For instance, two bucks will seldom look directly into each other's eyes when displaying in this manner, unless a fight is imminent. It's almost as if they are displaying their antlers and superb physique as they watch each other out of the corner of their eyes. Each buck seems to be hoping to ward off his opponent by appearing rougher and tougher.

Mule Deer Fights

Fights are quite common among mule deer bucks in the rut, especially in areas where the doe population is limited and the breeding competition keen. I see many broken antlers on our ranch, both during and after the rut. A serious mule deer fight is a sobering event to witness, as both combatants are generally ruthless. Imagine about 500 total pounds of deer shoving, lunging and gouging each other with absolutely no concern for anything but wiping out their opponent. They go at it in a big way, but the system works because the best one wins and gets the doe.

JVN

Deer Talk

To observe a group of totally relaxed mule deer, just going about their business, is a lesson in how much vocal communication really goes on. My first such encounter was in a northern Utah canyon, after my brother Chuck and I bellied up over the edge and began to glass it from behind a juniper. The first hint that anything was alive in the stone-quiet drainage was a sheep-like "blat," then a lower-pitched call back. Immediately a doe and her fawn stepped out, across from us and perhaps two hundred yards away. Then the side of the canyon seemed to come alive with a dozen deer browsing nonchalantly through the junipers, totally relaxed in the late-afternoon shadows. We heard blats, baa's, mews and what seemed like a chirp or two. Fascinated, we listened to it all, trying to decipher what they were saying and holding back a few chuckles at the variety of sounds. If there was a buck there, we missed it, spending most of our time taking advantage of this rare peek into the world of totally undisturbed mule deer.

TJC

Observe this doe-fawn group quietly and you're sure to hear them "talking" back and forth.

Social Rank

Mule deer, as does most wildlife, have a pecking order within their social group. This is true in both the doe/fawn groups, and the buck groups of summer and early autumn. There is always a lead doe or dominant buck in the group who puts up with very little "guff" from any of the other deer. These lead deer will strike with a front foot, butt with their head or antlers, or kick any other group member who gets out of line. Ways of getting out of line include things like being the first deer to an especially delicious patch of browse, or being in a nice shady spot when the sun swings around and obliterates the lead deer's patch of comfort. These high-ranking deer earn their keep though, as they usually lead the pack when it comes to detecting and fleeing danger.

But these high-ranking deer, often the older and more mature animals, will sometimes take up the rear or drag position when the group is fleeing danger or traveling from one drainage to another. These dominant deer will sometimes even coax (often with an antler), the younger and more inexperienced of the group to go first. Keep this in mind if you get the opportunity to watch a bunch of bucks filing through a spot one-by-one.

Predators

Predators play a major role in every mule deer's life and in overall herd numbers in any given area. Main mule deer predators include mountain lions, bobcats, wolves and coyotes. Mountain lions have made a comeback in the West, and the big cats definitely take their fair share of muleys, often at will it seems. Bobcats are strong, efficient hunters despite their relatively small size, and will take a mule deer fawn whenever they can. Where they've made comebacks, wolves pressure mule deer fairly heavily. But in this day and age, it is the coyote that affects mule deer populations most severely. Coyotes are sly, smart and formidable predators. When coyote populations are allowed to grow to high densities, they can severely reduce mule deer fawn production and populations.

Bucks start young when it comes to establishing their rank in the social order.

Coyotes are efficient mule deer predators.

Coyotes First-Hand

Although they take down many full grown animals, coyotes do the most damage to fawn crops in the spring and early summer. In my neck of the woods in early summer you can see six or seven does running together, each with a fawn or two. By fall, the same doe group may have only one fawn, that's a TOTAL of one fawn, tagging along. Coyotes know when they see a doe off by herself in the spring, she has a fawn somewhere nearby. I've seen them "camp" on a single doe, laying around and watching her all day from a safe distance, knowing full well she will have to leave the fawn and go to water sooner or later. Then it's good-bye fawn.

One time I watched nine coyotes hunt a particular draw all at once. Two waited at the end of the draw for anything fleeing and the rest worked back and forth, like bird dogs, flushing anything in hiding. I have also watched three coyotes chase a full grown doe towards two other coyotes in hiding. Lucky for her she got away. That day.

Coyotes are very good at what they do and that's not a problem. It only becomes a problem when coyote populations are allowed to grow to high densities. Their only recourse to feed the pack is to hunt harder and kill more deer. How to control coyotes when fur prices are down, and varmint hunters and trappers aren't concentrating on them, is a real problem. Even when a certain coyote population gets hunted extra hard, they make up for the decline with huge litters of pups the next spring.

Coyotes will inhabit the earth long after man is gone. Coyotes are necessary in the whole scheme of things and I'm not one to wish for their extinction. But while out in the boonies, take a coyote any chance you get. (Be sure it's legal at that particular time of year and with the license you hold, and that you won't be scaring away a big buck.) Coyotes are survivors and can easily withstand the hunting pressure, and you will save some mule deer fawns. You might even get a decent fur.

JVN

The Mule Deer Attitude

In general, mule deer are reasonably laid back, except for the bigger and more experienced bucks. These bucks know they're in great demand. Even from a predator's point of view, such as a mountain lion, a single loner buck (usually a big one) is much easier to stalk than several does or a group of bucks with its many noses, eyes and ears. So those "loner" bucks are pursued more often and have more paranoid attitudes as a result of many close calls and successful escapes.

The docile attitudes of most younger mule deer does and bucks, including the fawns, are more than likely the reasons mule deer have mistakenly been given the reputation for being a pushover when hunting season rolls around. In many hunting areas, does are not allowed to be taken, so most of their encounters with humans are fairly uneventful. This gives them a sense of security within a reasonable distance of a human. Even if a buck (often a young one) is taken among the does and fawns, no harm

The Disappearing Couple

As of this writing, there are two particular old bucks on our place that I have seen now for about five years. Each was mature when I first discovered him. As of three years ago, one has only three points on each side and the other only two points on each antler; but both have an honest 30-inch spread. Their antlers obviously have regressed, as all mule deer antlers do when the buck passes his prime.

Some of my clients, who have taken large bucks in the past, participate in an effort to take some of these older bucks. This would allow some of the younger big bucks to get bigger. We have specifically hunted these Wyoming bucks for three years now. I prepare by watching them regularly from great distances before the season in order to plan a strategy. We have yet to even see them during the rifle season. Yet after the season, when the rut begins, they are right back in their normal range. Where these gray ghosts go, and how they know when to disappear, remains a mystery. They just vanish.

I suspect they'll die of old age, and I probably won't find them even then.

JVN

Mule Deer Tricks

Although whitetails are generally considered the masters of evasion, I have had mule deer complete every single one of those so-called whitetail tricks on me. Just one example is circling a hunter who is doing a push through cover. Once, in Utah's steep and brushy Wellsville Mountains, I was hunting through an unbelievably thick, high-country brush patch. My goal was to roust a buck out to my two waiting partners. I would hear deer circling around me, standing up and walking off to the side, or taking a couple hops uphill and then stopping. But I never saw them. They certainly weren't going to leave the cover. These deer were not dumb. They were calm and collected, and they seemed to know what was up. They weren't going to leave that brush patch, no matter how many times I traipsed through.

TJC

came to them and they may soon be back to their old unconcerned selves.

There are exceptions to this rule. Some of the older does, who have seen many-a hunting season or are raised in country where extreme predation takes place, are as hard to find, sneak up on (or sneak past) as the big bucks are. Many-a wily old doe has foiled even the best laid plans.

Once you've had an opportunity to chase a more educated big buck you will soon dismiss any notion of mule deer being a pushover. A buck just doesn't get to be four, five or more years old by hanging loose. He stays calm in the face of danger, there's no doubt about that, but that is probably what saves his skin time and time again. See the sidebars at left for some examples.

Habitat Types

To dive into detailed descriptions of each of the mule deer's habitats would take up much of a good-sized book. What we will say is this: What's most fascinating about the whole matter is the wide variety of habitats a mule deer calls home, and how adaptable the animal is. A mule deer's climate tolerance is equal to or better than that of any other mammal. You'll find mule deer in sweltering Arizona heat, bitter British Columbia cold, wind-whipped Colorado flatlands, parched New Mexico deserts and many places in between. You'll find muleys on mountain peaks and mountain sides, as well as in foothills, prairies, badlands, deserts, agricultural areas and river bottoms. Their range is approximately 1,550 miles long by 930 miles wide and they are found from the southern Yukon to northern Mexico. The chapter *Mule Deer State by State* will give you a good idea where to find them.

Mule deer on the prairie.

Classic, high-mountain mule deer country.

Typical pinyon-juniper habitat.

Food And Feeding, And Water

It's probably easier to list what a mule deer won't eat rather than itemizing a complete list of what they do eat. Mule deer are browsers, and have adapted to eat over 700 different plants. Like most animals, they will be found in the areas where the best feed and some water exist.

One of the most important staples during winter is sagebrush; it is high in protein, and usually tall enough so that deer can get at the nutritious leaves and buds even when there's some snow on the ground.

In dry country, try taking a stand around a water source. In this case, a windmill provides essential water for prairie deer.

A Rancher's Perspective

My grandfather used to say, "You can always tell which field is the best in the summer, and which haystack is the best in the winter, by taking note of which ones the deer are working on!" Mule deer are selective feeders and the majority of the population, in any given area, will be found where the "grub" is the best. The exception is when a little hunting pressure shows up, in which case the more experienced bucks will pull back and are apt to be found in some of the most isolated areas where neither water nor food are easily available. And then they'll only go to water every couple of days, and feed on what is available around their hiding spot at night.

Livestock graze and generally feed on different kinds of plants than mule deer, which browse. So the two will inhabit the same areas with little, if any, impact upon each other as long as range management of the livestock takes into consideration wildlife needs. If the livestock over-graze, mule deer will move on to where the best feed is, even if it is several miles away. A prudent ranch manager who enjoys the many benefits of wildlife will plan his livestock grazing strategies accordingly.

But I have noticed that when I move a bunch of cows into a pasture (understand that a pasture in the West can cover thousands of acres) that harbors deer, the larger bucks will move into an adjacent pasture where there are no cattle. I believe these older bucks don't like the extra commotion with cows and calves bawling and us driving through regularly checking water and salt. Once we rotate the cattle into the adjacent pasture, the larger bucks move back into the pasture they originally came from. Again, I believe, to avoid the commotion.

JVN

The Seasons

In some parts of muley country, the deer spend the winter and summer in the same general area. But for the most part, mule deer have fairly specific winter and summer ranges. Sometimes these ranges are a relatively short distance apart, maybe only a few thousand feet of elevation, as the deer vacate the now-harsh high country in favor of milder weather and easier living in the foothills. Some herds may travel many miles. For example, they may head from the windward slopes of a mountain range to the leeward side, or from wind-battered high plains to the breaks of a major river drainage. Snow, wind and cold are the elements that drive deer from summer range to winter range.

Early summer, mule deer doe and fawn.

The Rut And The Next Generation

Before all that snow flies, mule deer complete their rutting season. The peak of rutting activity varies greatly by region. In most of the West, mid- to late-November sees the most activity. In general, the mule deer rut peaks a bit earlier than the whitetail rut and the muley bucks compete just as heavily for does (see the communications section of this chapter and the sidebar there).

An interesting fallacy that many folks believe is that the biggest and toughest bucks gather harems of does to defend. While it's true you'll see a buck hanging with a group of does, it's only because the does are in their normal grouping of deer. The buck is there with them, hanging around and going where they go and waiting for some of the females to come into estrous. He'll fight off other bucks trying to horn in, but only to defend his right to be there.

It takes a lot of energy to make it through the breeding season. After the rut, if a big buck has worked himself too hard, he might not live through the winter. But even after a buck dies, he lives on if the doe is tough enough to survive the rigors of the season. That buck's sons and daughters are born the next May and June when the country is greening up and lush once again.

This buck is really enjoying his whiff of doe-in-heat. A biologist would call it flehmening.

Rattle & Grunt 'Em Up

Believe it or not, "rattling" a mule deer up close during the rut works fairly well. It's not a very common tactic, as most areas don't have open seasons in the rut. But rattling can be accomplished much in the same manner as with a white-tailed deer. You can also rattle a mule deer in, with some success, during and shortly after they rub the velvet from their antlers. This works best by rattling with a gentler technique than the normal, aggressive rattling.

Don't ignore grunt calls either. Mule deer are vocal animals, and a properly-placed "uurp" can slow down or attract a buck on the prowl.

Mule deer bucks get aggressive during the rut, and will take it out on available woody vegetation such as this scrub cedar.

Chapter 3
Talking the Western Lingo

Before we start discussing where to look to find mule deer using the images outlined in Chapter 4, there is some "lingo" you must be able to understand and use in order to be considered a true trophy mule deer hunter.

This technical array of legendary vocabulary includes words like draw, wash-out, cut-bank, hogback, overhang, finger and several other terms commonly used in mule deer country. Those of you with a dazzling command of the English language may find this section a bit confusing! But with a little practice you'll soon fit right in.

You'll need to know this jargon so you can understand what and where we are talking about. You'll also need this knowledge to know and see what we mean once you are in the field. It's also important to speak the same language as your guide, if you happen to hire one. (Note: Arguing with your guide or outfitter over the validity of these terms is not recommended. Such debate could earn you a stint of several days in what is commonly known as "the penalty stand" or you could be the victim of a "Schooner Canyon" death march!)

And it doesn't hurt to talk like a local if you're hunting on your own and have the good fortune to be visiting with some people asking for advice on where and how to hunt.

Drainage: A general term that describes any sort of watershed. A main canyon and a prairie valley are drainages, for instance.

Canyon: A steep-sided, main drainage that starts at the top of a mountain or high area and opens up far below. Think of it as a very steep-sided valley, or a gorge.

In the mountains, canyons start high and are relatively small. But they steadily grow as they proceed downslope.

Draw: A valley of any size or description. It can be considered to be the main drainage or any side fork of the main drainage. The Grand Canyon, to some folks, is just a big "draw"!

Main draw with side-draw fingers. Bucks prefer to bed in the finger draws, so be sure to hunt them hard.

Wash-out: A place where, over time, water has cut a ditch in the earth. This ditch can be referred to as a washout regardless of size, as long as it doesn't exceed the size of a draw.

Here's an example of a wash-out. You'll find mule deer bucks right in the bottom.

Cut-bank: Any kind of dirt cliff at the end of a wash-out or eroded area. This exposed dirt cliff can measure from six inches high to as large as you can imagine. The key words here are "dirt" and "cliff."

Well-used mule deer bed under a cut-bank.

Hogback: A hill, peninsula or ridge between two drainages, draws or washouts. To better understand, picture a hog standing, facing you, and then picture the shape of his back. This term can be used for any size hill, peninsula or ridge. (Could also describe someone's mother in law!)

Overhang: A rock or dirt cliff, hanging out over any part of earth, creating a roof (so to speak) where shade and shelter is present for a major portion of the day. Hangover is not a synonym.

Muley doe bedded under an overhang.

Fingers: Small lines of brush or timber stretching out from a main patch of brush or timber. Or, fingers can be smaller washouts, hogbacks, draws or drainages that branch out from the main entities.

Scrub cedar: Small cedar trees or any other small tree of comparable size and shape, including piñon or juniper. The accuracy of horticultural terms matters very little when talking to most Western folks or pointing out a big monster buck in the heat of the moment!

Rockpile: A bunch of rocks in a pile, a few scattered rocks fairly close together, or a huge out-cropping of rocks the size of a hotel. Again the term is used rather loosely.

Gully: A gully can be any sort of valley, large or small, in the earth.

Crick: (Easterners might call this a "creek.") The word can refer to anything from a trickle of water to a raging river. To fully understand the lingo you must understand that a crick can also be any kind of drainage, whether it has water in it or not! Although a crick is generally thought of as actually having running water, it could mean anything that might have had water once, sometime, back to the beginning of time. So if you have a guide and he says, "Go up the crick," that means stay in the main drainage (if there is no water) or stay along the water's edge.

Snag: An old dead bush or tree which can be standing or lying down. Unless you're in the town pub and are approached by a very homely man or woman do not use this term loosely!

Dark timber: Any heavily brushed or heavily timbered north slope where the "bogeyman" lives. It's also where monster mule deer go to hide and never be found. This is the kind of timber that makes you look behind yourself more than usual.

Some dark timber.

Quakies or quakers: Really aspen or birch trees. But any trees that have round, green leaves in late summer that turn yellow in the fall could be commonly referred to as "quakies." Quakies are generally found where there is a spring or the ground water is very close to the surface. Lush vegetation and good cover is normally associated with their presence and mule deer are very aware of this.

Slide: Generally found in the mountains, a slide can be any long, steep opening that divides a patch of timber. To be a slide, the opening must appear to have had an avalanche of mud, rocks or snow pass through it.

Ridge: Any short- or long-running piece of real estate that divides any kind of watershed, large or small.

Saddle: A low point or dip in a ridge. You could cross a ridge at a saddle and get into the next draw or drainage without having to climb the ridge's full height.

Basin: A gently sloping or flat area, on a mountain or in a range of hills. Liken it to standing in a wash basin. There are steep slopes all around, but where you are the terrain is gentle or even flat.

When you hear and can reasonably comprehend something like the following (or say it with reasonable confidence) you're well on your way to becoming an honest-to-gosh trophy mule deer hunter:

"Did you see that buck? He come out of that draw over there, jumped up that cut-bank on the north side of that narrow hogback, ducked under the reddish overhang, went up the pine tree finger right there and stopped by that last scrub cedar. When he turned around for a last look, I 'bout fell over backwards! From there, he went just south of that rockpile, the little one by that old snag , through those quakies across the crick and up that gully where he slipped into that patch of dark timber. Then he crossed over in that little saddle and dropped into the next drainage. Man, I m tellin' ya, he was a monster!"

Note From A Native

The Western language, at best, is sometimes mind boggling, often vaguely descriptive, and at times makes little sense. But what's important is it's always truly colorful! And, like any language, the names for certain features and plants will change with the region, state and locale. Glad to be of such invaluable assistance.

JVN

Chapter 4

Seeing the Gray Ghost— What to Look for

Spotting Mule Deer: Look For Pieces & Parts

As discussed in the introduction, to be a successful trophy mule deer hunter it is critical to locate deer long before they see you. Glassing and spotting with optics, the techniques of which are covered in subsequent chapters, is the number one consideration for successfully hunting mule deer country.

This chapter will show and tell you what to look for. You need to know what to look for because Muleys can truly become gray ghosts of the sage, grass, rimrock, quakies, lodgepole or any terrain they inhabit.

Mule deer bucks select places to rest and bed that are, in most cases, well-hidden yet provide a panoramic view. A big buck's general tendency is to hole up in a position where he can see a lot of country, and sneak out far ahead of imminent danger. If not well-hidden, the spot will instead take full advantage of the deer's superior eyes, nose, ears and protective coloration. In either case, where a mature mule deer buck beds is carefully chosen, stra-tegically located and unlikely to offer you a noise-free, scent-free or entirely invisible route to the deer. To have any chance of successfully approaching to within range you have to see him first.

Think about it for a minute. Say you had nothing to do but lie in the shade where you had a nice view. You also wore a coat the color of your surroundings and possessed superior eyes which offer fantastic peripheral vision. Let's also give you two huge, swiveling ears that gather every clink, clatter, swish and other sound coming from the surrounding countryside. You are now much like a U.S. Navy submarine: silent, nearly invisible and watching the radar and sonar for any movement or sounds! Plus, let's say you also know how to choose a position and orient yourself so that the wind warns your sensitive nose of any dangers you can't see or hear. What would be the chances of anything approaching unnoticed? Slim, to say the least.

How do you see mule deer before they detect you? You have to know how to approach. Stay under the radar (out of sight). Minimize the reception of sonar (make very little noise). And avoid the nose (hunt with the wind in your face).

Despite the importance of hearing and smelling, detecting movement by sight is a mule deer buck's number one defense. This chapter will help you develop the necessary skills to be a true cut above the rest in seeing mule deer before they see you.

Know What To Look For

The first key is knowing what to look for. When glassing for mule deer, don't concern yourself with spotting the whole deer at once. Generally you will have a picture of an entire deer engraved in your mind and will seldom glass over one out in the open. Learn instead to focus your attention on images representing what we call "pieces and parts" of mule deer. There are 16 images described in detail in this chapter. Train your mind to alert your eyes to "snap to" and look again when you spot one of these images.

These images will become your basis for spotting more mule deer in any type of habitat. Burn these pieces and parts into your mind's eye, then concentrate on them and let them help you spot mule deer you might have otherwise looked past.

A Lifetime Of Spotting Mule Deer

I have always had a special ability to spot mule deer. Even when I was a kid, my father's hunting companions would remark, "Man that kid has good eyes!" Turns out that my eyes were really no sharper than anyone else's. I just didn't realize what was happening visually, until years later.

Having spent considerable time reading various documents in an early career, my eyesight seemed to be getting worse. So I went to the eye doctor and was fitted with a pair of glasses. I couldn't believe the detail I could then see! Hunting season was not far away and I thought, "I'll see every hidden buck within miles!" But to my surprise, I had a heck of a time seeing deer before my hunting partners did that season.

Upon close examination I realized that I was seeing too much detail! This caused my "eye-to-mind" coordination (a skill I'd unknowingly developed over the years) to become confused. All that new detail caused me to "snap to" constantly on images that were irrelevant. Once I took my glasses off, I was right back to my old mule deer "decoding" self.

Therein lies the key. There are millions of images out there in the sage, timber, sand, grass, rocks and pucker brush. Don't drive yourself crazy picking each aspect apart. Just concentrate on certain images, the ones described in this chapter. It's not extremely important to see these images clearly, but it is important to "key" on them and then slow down enough to pick apart anything resembling them. It will take some practice, but by memorizing these images to the point of blocking out all other landscape and foliage distractions, you'll find more mule deer.

These are the images that have brought me 33 years of success finding mule deer, long before they saw me. I've used them to find trophy mule deer bucks for myself and my family, as well as dozens of visiting clients. You'll find a graphic rendition of each, a photograph indicating a real life example, and some brief coaching on what you're looking for and why.

JVN

Image #1: Two-Branch Antler

This image takes the number one spot for two reasons. Not only is it one of the most prominent thoughts on our minds while scanning for trophy mule deer, but it's also a very common element or part to see first. Why? Although mule deer bucks generally hide themselves quite well, they don't seem to have a good feel for how far their antlers rise up above their eye level.

It's common to be glassing and find a set of horns sticking out of the brush long before you see the body of the deer. Antlers' importance as a prime piece or part can also be attributed to the mule deer's tendency to bed in the shade. As the shade begins to dissipate in the morning, the first deer part to receive the sun is generally the antlers. A buck will continue to lie in that spot (with his head gear sticking out) until the sun gets to his eye level or becomes a bother to other parts of his body. Conversely, as the sun drops in the evening, a buck's bedding spot before his evening feed may provide shade for his body, but leave his antlers up in the sun until the shadows grow over them.

Note that the photos in this section may be slightly out of focus to assist in learning to look for images rather than just clearly visible deer.

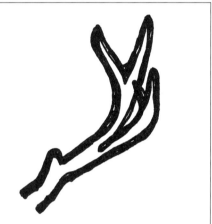

A Note On Antler Color

The color of antlers plays a large role in being able to pick them out. Take note of the various types of vegetation in your hunting area. Mule deer antlers will vary in color depending on the types of vegetation they use to rub the velvet off. The antlers of mountain-country mule deer are dark compared to those of deer on the prairies or in the desert, because of the pitch in pine trees. There are other genetic and nutritional factors involved here also, but the trees and brush in an area can give you an idea of what coloration to expect.

Once you've seen a few bucks in an area you'll know what to look for. To get a head start, ask the locals before you start your hunt. You may get a strange look at first, but what kind of hunter doesn't like to talk about antlers?

Velvet coloration varies considerably between deer in the same area. As a rule of thumb, a younger deer's velvet is light brown while the older deer's velvet tends to be more of a chocolate brown.

In general, look for the typical branched configuration of mule deer antlers – two points on the upper beam and two on the lower or main beam. There will be time to count all the points once you've confirmed it's a deer. Just concentrate on the main frame as outlined.

Always glass for just one antler. Where there's one there's customarily another, but looking for one makes the work simpler. Plus— if you're always looking for two antlers you may miss a well-hidden buck, as your mind will picture only a few configurations in which those two antlers should be facing. In reality there are hundreds of directions for mule deer to lay, so don't give your mind a chance to dismiss any possibility.

Antlers have a shine with some rubbed white hues, especially when in the sun. This smooth, polished look contrasts with the duller look of brush and branches. Even in the shade, antlers look smoother. So watch for contrasts.

Bowhunters and other early-season hunters note that antlers in velvet are much harder to see because their "fuzzy" appearance blends better into the surroundings. But again, concentrate on the main frame and you'll pick them out anyway. See the sidebar for more thoughts on bucks in velvet

Note also that backdrops have a tendency to outline or highlight an antler. Lighter backdrops outline, while darker backdrops highlight. Again, contrast is one of the keys.

You can find an antler "sticking out" in any number of places. We'll explore where to look later.

Image #2: The Triangle – Dark Forehead Patch, Eyes And Black Nose

Always keep an eye open for these components. The dark forehead patch, eyes and black nose make up a rough upside-down triangle.

Many times, because of the terrain or vegetation in which a deer chooses to bed (some types of sage look white from a distance, white aspen or birch tree trunks, and snow cover), you won't always see a buck's white face first. In such cases the black of this triangle tends to jump out at you. The dark elements can be picked out easily against such backgrounds. Again, key on the configuration.

If you find what appears to be one element, begin "rooting around" with your optics until you find the other two. Mule deer eyes have what appears to be a white eyebrow above each eye. The nose generally has two white spots, one just underneath each nostril. The forehead patch or "buck's mask" appears all black from a distance, but when examined closely begins with black on the bridge of the nose and between the eyes, then turns grayish brown, gray or sometimes even almost white,

depending on the age of the buck, as it sweeps over the top of the head.

Sounds like a lot of trouble. But if you learn each of these components and the configuration they create, you'll spot many more mule deer, even in heavy cover.

Image #3: Mule Ears

The ears are among the mule deer's most prominent features and, not surprisingly, are some of most common pieces and parts you'll find while glassing. For this particular image though, look only for the shape that you would create drawing a solid line from the tip of one ear, down across the top of the ear to the forehead, across the forehead and up to the tip of the other ear. This upper line, as de-scribed, is the component to key on. For con-firmation, look for the rounded underside of each ear.

This image stands out quite well in most any kind of terrain, but you have to be on the look-out for it. It's fairly easy to pass over, as it's just a line. In image number ten we will examine the individual mule deer ear in depth includ-ing its shape, lines and color.

Respect The Does And Fawns

Although it's true you'll find more does and fawns with this image than bucks, that in itself can be of major im-portance. I've had many-a cagey old doe sound the "stumble bum" alert (blow her nose) and warn all the deer in the immediate area of my mistake. It's far better to find does and fawns, all of them, before they find you and blow your chances at any bucks in the area.

JVN

Image #4: South End Of A Northbound Mule Deer

The mule deer's rump is quite noticeable in most terrain types and cover. There is plenty of visual competition for your eyes when it comes to spotting mule deer rumps, and here is the tip for quickly deciding if the image might have a mule deer attached and therefore deserves more of your attention.

To confirm that a mule deer is hooked to what you're looking at, there should be a black spot toward the bottom of the white. That black spot, common to all mule deer, is the tip of the tail. The tip will resemble an artist's paintbrush, wide at the base of the bristles and tapered to a fine point. There are a few mule deer without a black tip but it's fairly uncommon. In addition to locating the black tip of the tail, remember that mule deer wag their tails often while feeding or in a relaxed state. That's another telltale sign.

When in the sun, the mule deer's rump shines like a beacon. In the shade it's a little easier to miss, especially if there's snow on the ground.

Many times when a deer is lying down, he will tuck his tail under himself, hiding the black tip. In this case all you'll find is a shiny white spot. As with all these images, it is then up to you to begin building the other components of the deer. Find the elbow joint in the hind leg, the upper thigh, the back line, and so forth, for confirmation.

Here's a buck without a black tip on his tail.

The Rump Giveaway

After catching my breath, I eased into the gloomy, brush-choked, north-facing fir timber. I had been a minute too late and about a hundred yards away from intercepting the group of Idaho muleys, buck included, that had fed through the sage and over the crest of the ridge at first light. But I knew I was only a minute behind and Jim Campbell of Wellsville, Utah, who I was hunting with, motioned me on in when I looked back across the draw at him.

After scanning the close-in quarters of the timber's second gully, I took a step to duck under a branch and stopped short, heart pounding, in mid-squat. What appeared to be a whitish-gray boulder, just 15 yards away, caught every wisp of my attention. In the gray-green gloom and thick brush, it took a minute to locate a black eye above what I knew to be a mule deer rump. Then an ear flicked. A black-tipped tail swished. I eased the rifle up, knowing it was a buck, but I could not see antlers. The deer moved off slowly and I never caught up again, but it was the beacon of the rump that snapped my attention into high gear and gave me the opportunity to observe the deer at spitting distance without taking another step into his view and spooking him.

Watching for rumps works in close, thick quarters as well as open, long-range ones.

TJC

Image #5: Basic Inside Antler Shape

Many times when glassing at great distances, all you have is a basic image like we're describing. The details are impossible to pick out. As discussed previously, antlers can be found sticking out above the skyline, outlined against lighter colored back drops, highlighted by darker backdrops or framed by vegetation. This is another antler image that should jump out at you readily, if you're in the proper mindset.

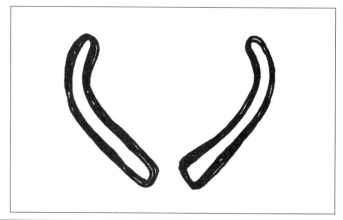

This image depicts the basic inside shape of a typical mule deer's antlers. Take a look sometime while glassing a buck at a great distance and note the shape. Picking out each individual point is impossible without a very powerful spotting scope. But the basic inside shape is easily recognized.

Note that this is a highly symmetrical, smooth-edged shape, graceful and often out-of-place in a sea of sage or astride a rocky, sharp-edged hillside.

True, a lot of vegetation, dead snags and bushes have a similar shape, but each image is worth closer scrutiny. Sometimes that old, dead snag you passed over jumps up and, attached to its mule deer owner, quits the country.

Image #6: The Fork (V)

This image can cause you to go nuts. Every tree, bush and branch has a fork of some sort. And so do antlers. But if you're going to be extremely good at trophy mule deer hunting, every fork or "V" you see deserves a closer look.

If nothing else, checking out each and every fork will slow your scanning, which allows you to see more deer in the long run. The fork or "V" will lead you to a goodly portion of that total.

So, as you're glassing, look for any kind of fork. Once you've found one, watch it for an extended period of time; maybe 30 seconds or so. If there's a buck under there, he'll generally make a small movement of some kind while fighting flies, flicking an ear, scratching an itch or turning to look at something that has caught his eye.

Begin trying to build the rest of the main frame of the antler around the fork as you keep an eye peeled for other mule deer components ... ears, forehead patch, eyes and so forth. The top fork of a buck's antler is usually the one sticking out of the cover. This fork is generally perpendicular to the ground with the "V" pointing down when a buck is laying with his head up. The fork on the main beam, however, is not generally perpendicular to the ground and is much harder to decipher from the many other "forks" you'll see as you scan the landscape and vegetation.

Key on this "V" shape and its proportions. The fingers of the "V" are normally uniform in length and the width of the "V" is not usually out of proportion to the length. There are always exceptions to the rule, but don't expect to see a "V" 15 inches wide with a tine length of only 5 inches. Well-proportioned forks are a good tip-off that it's something besides the branch of a tree or bush. Further study could turn up the buck of a lifetime.

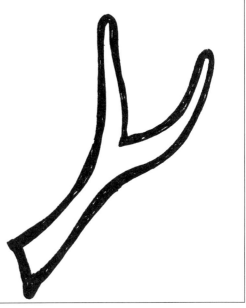

Image #7: White Face And Muzzle

White is a color that your eyes will easily pick up in your optics in most any terrain. A mule deer buck's muzzle is fairly white in the summer and early fall, but then turns extremely white with the buck's winter coat of gray. If a mule deer is well-hidden, sometimes the only thing to betray him is his stark white face. This element is one of the top three images to key on. Whenever your eyes and optics are in action, keep this image near the top of your list.

As with some of the other images discussed, there are components you must associate with the white face to confirm that it's a buck deer. These components include the black eye spots, dark forehead, black nose, white spots under the nostrils and white throat patch. In addition, always look for the beginning of antlers (see image number 3 in this chapter).

When a buck is facing directly toward you, the black eye spots or black nose are sometimes the first face elements you'll put together (as in image number 2), appearing to be the start of a "smiley face" in a patch of white. From head-on you might also see the white throat patch with a black circle (the nose) toward the top/center. From that throat patch up, begin "building" a buck's face and head with the other components.

Note how stark these bucks' white faces are, in comparison to the terrain.

Learning the basics of any skill can be tedious, so let's take a short pause. Study these bucks and break them down into the pieces and parts discussed thus far.

Bucks In Tuxedos

I often refer to mule deer bucks as having an "exalted tuxedo look." Their stark white faces, white throat patches and black nose "bow ties," along with those awesome racks tipped back, just seem to demand our respect. For me, there's nothing more exhilarating than to glass into a coulee and jerk my binoculars to a halt on three or four "exalted tuxedos," complete with massive headgear, glaring from their shadowy hideout.

JVN

Image #8: Legs

Typical mule deer habitat is full of objects that stick up perpendicular to the ground, but few of these things are tightly bunched with no branches.

From a great distance legs will appear to be three or four toothpicks protruding from the ground. Sometimes all you can see are two sticks, one behind the other, possibly with an angle in both (the two hind legs). A mule deer's legs are very light in color compared to most other parts of its body. This is especially true of the inside of the legs. So, when up against a dark backdrop, legs will stand out fairly well even when the upper body may blend in. Many times you'll spot a set of legs before seeing any other part of the deer. That's simply because they're what stands out best in many situations. Learn to key on them.

Again—once you key on the image, start building the other components. Work from the hoof and dew claw (if you're really close) up to the normal taper of a deer's leg, to the knee, to the bottom of the chest or belly and so on.

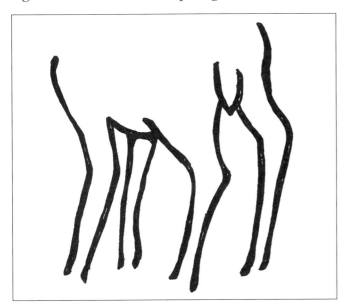

Horizontal Lines

Any whitetail hunter worth his salt knows about looking for horizontal lines. Use this image when looking for mule deer, too. In the sage, in the grasslands, in the brush of a canyon-bottom tangle... a horizontal line should really snap you to attention. Then, start looking for the leg components as described.

Key on continuous, smooth lines – it could be a mule deer belly or back – because they are out of place amongst the straight-trunked quakies, or out in the tall grass or chaparral.

TJC

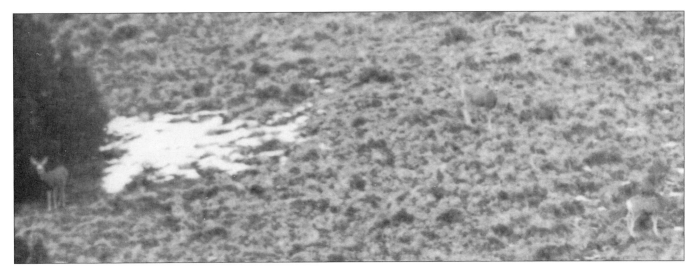

Image #9: Hind Leg, Laying Position

While glassing, pay attention to hard 90-degree angles. These angles are often created by the lower hind leg and the thigh of a bedded deer. Mule deer will also frequently lay with their hind legs sprawled out (especially the outside leg), creating a different look but following the same "hard angle" idea. There are right and left angles, depending on which direction the deer is laying. The length of this inside line, through the angle, is abnormal in most vegetation. So again, stop and investigate any "clean geometry" in the landscape.

Also, the rounded nature of the stifle joint (located between the upper and lower thigh) is an image that should commonly draw your attention. It resembles the "drumstick" of a chicken or turkey standing perpendicular to the ground.

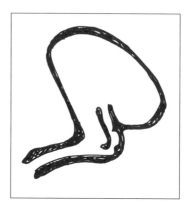

Image #10: Ear Lining And Outline

Mule deer ears have a very unique shape. Try to think of the ears as resembling candle flames being blown horizontally in a breeze. You could also think of them as large, broad leaves. In the sunlight, you'll note the gray outline and inner lining of white, if the deer is facing you. Also, the white line designating the top inside of the ear (an accent line if you will), is a clue that should make you take a second look.

In addition, there is a gray "ear flap" next to the skull with a noticeably whiter accent line on the bottom side. In the shade however, an ear will simply appear to be a large, broad leaf with that unique candle flame shape.

Images number 3 and number 10 may overlap a bit, but its important to break down the various components of a mule deer so you can become more proficient at finding each part, especially when the deer are well-hidden.

Image #11: Hind Leg, Vertical Position

While standing, the hind leg of any four-legged mammal has an interesting and out-of-place shape, and mule deer are no exception. From the shin bone to the elbow or hock up to the hip joint, a definite unique line can be drawn. Again, this particular line is unusual in most all vegetation and terrain. Cue on the angle at the elbow or hock. Then build components from the stifle joint to the hip joint and rump. Now, you don't have to get the dictionary out to understand terms like "stifle." All you're really looking for is that "snap to" line of a hind leg, clear up to where it hooks on to the body. Also note that the lower leg is generally much lighter in color than the upper part.

Image #12: Outside Antler Image And Top Of The Ears

Once again, there is some overlap with this image and some others, but keep in mind we are keying on different aspects of the image. It's important to watch for each one. Who knows which one will lead you to your next (or first) big mule deer buck.

This outside antler image, with the top line of the ears just beneath, is often the only deer-related image you'll pick up, especially when the buck is against a backdrop of dark brush or is standing or bedded in deep shade. In this case, the details of the antlers are hard to distinguish so an outline is all you'll see. Key on the graphic angle or gap created by the space between the bottom line of the antler and the top line of the ear. This image is normally presented when the deer is in a relaxed state.

Image #13: Side View Of The Face

With this image, key on the configuration of the eye, dark forehead patch, mouth line and nose. The long "snout" shape of the white muzzle with its black tip (the nose) is readily noticeable. In addition, most mule deer sport a heavy black line at the back of the chin; this line is perpendicular to and below the mouth. Also watch for the coal black oval of a deer's eye with its dark preorbital gland, all surrounded by a white ring. Finally, from the side, a dark forehead patch may appear to be an eyebrow. With a little practice these components should easily draw your attention.

You'll normally concentrate on this particular facial image and its components when hunting in heavy cover situations.

Image #14: Circles And Cylinders

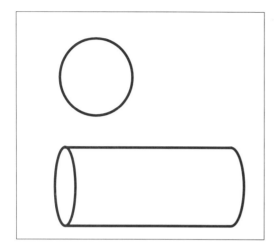

Whenever you see a circle, whether you're looking with the naked eye or with optics, stop and look it over carefully. At intermediate and long distances, whole mule deer as well as their the rump patches show up as circles. Don't bypass anything that has a cylinder shape either because, likewise at intermediate and long distances, a mule deer's body can appear cylinder shaped when you eliminate all the other parts. Although these two images are somewhat generic, they will account for about one-third of your long distance mule deer discoveries.

Image #15: Ears Back Position

This image, in relation to all other ear poses, will be the one you'll see most often when spotting a bedded deer. For the most part you'll see this image on small bucks before you pick out their antlers, and on does. This image consists of the top outline of two ears, rather close together and laid slightly back. This ear configuration is seen when the deer is totally relaxed, maybe even asleep and bedded facing away, broadside or quartering away.

Although the smaller bucks and does are not your ultimate objective here, remember that they can stir things up pretty good if spooked. That will blow your chances at the big buck just up the canyon. And, if you're hunting during the rut, where there are does there will be bucks lurking nearby.

This ear configuration will account for a big percentage of all the bedded mule deer you'll find.

Image #16: Shiny Spots

One more element to always keep your eyes open for is a shiny spot. In and of itself, a shiny spot can't be associated with any one shape or image. Rather, a shine or sheen is a key element of many of the images described, and is often the "snap to" indicator you need to slow down and check out a particular spot in detail.

As with many mammals, a mule deer's hair glistens in the proper light. And don't forget antlers; a glint of Western sun off a shiny, ivory-like tine has given away the hiding spot of many-a mule deer buck. Shiny spots will take on many shapes and glassing over them is a mistake.

The three shiny spots in the center of this scene should grab your attention right away. Can you find the other two muleys as well?

Another shiny spot glistening in the sunlight ... a dead giveaway to a mule deer's presence.

The Right Proportions

Another very important aspect of this entire concept is proportion. Any good outfitter or guide, for any species, will tell you that it's extremely important to have a concept of the animal's proportion in relation to its surroundings while glassing. One of the first things I asked Harry Dodge of Pinnell and Talifson, a good brown bear guide I had in Alaska, was, "How do you tell a big bear from a mediocre bear?" He answered, "You compare them to the terrain, rocks, trees, stumps and bushes. Things you have a good feel for the size of."

So when you find a mule deer, wherever you choose to hunt, compare the deer and the various image components to the surrounding elements of his domain. It will take a day or so for your depth perception to get adjusted. Before long, you'll not only have a feel for the size of a mule deer in relation to his habitat but will also have a feel for the size of each component, in relation to that particular habitat.

JVN

Remember "FERAL"

Now we've thrown a lot of information at you all at once. There truly are a lot of images to remember to look for, but here's a tip to help you recall the "core" of this technique, the acronym FERAL.

You've probably noticed that our images really only consist of a few major deer parts and then pieces of each. Those major parts are: Faces, Ears, Rumps, Antlers and Legs (FERAL). Remember these parts, and the key elements of what to look for will always be mentally handy.

Conclusion

Memorize the core images and their associated components and you'll spot mule deer long before the average hunter. You'll locate bucks you otherwise would have missed. By burning these images into your mind it becomes second nature for you to "snap to" when any of them are encountered. No matter whether you see them with the naked eye or with optics: look again and check it out!

Now it takes some time for these images to register automatically between your eyes and your mind. But with practice you'll be surprised how quickly you will pick them up. If you don't live in mule deer country, you can practice this technique on whitetails all year long.

For example: when you spot a deer in a field or even where the animal is partially hidden, mentally break the deer down into components of the images we've specified here. Concentrate on each one separately and study the components of each image thoroughly. This process will at least get you started on learning to key on images (pieces and parts) and not the whole deer.

If you don't have an opportunity to do this before you venture out in mule deer country, trace a copy of these "pieces & parts" images and stick it in your pocket. Then, while you're hunting mule deer, review the images regularly, especially when you find a deer and have an opportunity to observe it for an extended period of time.

We've crammed a lot of detail into this chapter. But it is precisely those details that will provide you with more mule deer hunting success. Review this information several times each year and you will soon find it to be second nature.

Check It All Out

I can't tell you how many times throughout the year I stop to check out images like those we've just described. Enough that my wife, during the summer, and my clients, during the fall, would like to throw up! As a rancher I'm outside with mule deer, either in my work with cattle or by actually stalking deer with a camera or weapon, almost every day of the year. Most of my experienced companions will tell you, "You can't get anywhere fast, because Jim can't go for too long without stopping to check out another suspicious-looking spot over there." My wife gets tired of it. My hunting clients eventually get tired of it, until I point out the deer of a lifetime!

JVN

Chapter 5

Seeing the Gray Ghost— Where to Look

Introduction

Now that you know what to look for while mule deer hunting and have received a vocabulary of appropriate geographical and botanical terms, along with other mule deer country lingo, it's time to discuss where to look for mule deer. As you'll see in this and the subsequent chapter, there's a lot more to locating mule deer than just walking out, plopping down and looking randomly around the countryside.

If there's one constant about mule deer country, it's that the terrain is invariably big. The mountains, with all their canyons and draws and basins and timber, are immense. Even their foothills seem to stretch on forever. The high sage deserts sprawl endlessly to the horizons. Piñon-juniper and scrub cedar habitats provide virtual mule deer mazes with nearly unlimited cover and countless bedding spots. Even the wide-open, rolling prairie, with all its folds and seams, provides thou-

sands of hidey holes for mule deer. Get into the prairie breaks draining to a major river and there's even more country for a mule deer to retreat to.

Having an educated guess on where to look —which is what this chapter provides— is going to save you time and effort. It will also help you find even more mule deer to observe and possibly stalk.

Notice we said mule deer, not just "trophy" mule deer. That's because it is very important to try to find <u>all</u> the mule deer in the area you're glassing. Does and small bucks are often the culprits that keep you from getting a crack at the big boys. And anyway, the more deer you find, the quicker you'll get good at the task. We will describe the most likely places to find a trophy buck, but don't ignore the small bucks and does; leaving them undisturbed may be one of the ultimate keys to your success.

A Shady Plan

When easing up to look over a new piece of country always begin glassing the shady areas first. Shade of any kind or size is the number one place to locate mule deer. We will talk about geography shortly. But if you can't remember anything else, look for mule deer in the shade! It's that simple. Whether it's early morning, midday or late evening; whether the deer are up and feeding or bedded down shade is their preference.

The biggest bucks will feed and bed in shade higher up on the edge of ridges, where they have a good view during the morning hours. This also allows them to take advantage of rising thermal currents as the day drags on. However, as the day heats up (remember, even a cool day heats up relative to a cold dawn) and the bucks' shade begins to dissipate up high,

they may head down into the deeper parts of washouts, draws, canyons, black timber and other out-of-the-way spots. They'll be seeking shade with more longevity.

The young bucks and does, as a loose, general rule, are found in the shade lower on the slopes and around the best feed and water. Not that big bucks can't be found in the best feed and close to water, but their tendencies are to visit these areas only very late in the day, and then leave quite early before first light the next day. Bigger, older bucks are just more reclusive; dusk, night and dawn provide the ultimate shade. Just after daylight is a great time to catch these older, more experienced bucks making the transition to their higher, shady bedding and feeding areas.

Big mule deer bucks like to bed in the shade. It's that simple.

Finding Shade

Most of us think of trees when we think shade. But in much of mule deer country, especially those areas where the big bucks retreat to, there might not be traditional forest-type cover. So, in general, where do you find shade?

Trees and tall Vegetation. We already mentioned trees. But don't assume there has to be a whole forest, or even a clump of trees. A single juniper, pine or cedar offers plenty of shade for a mule deer buck. Even big sage or other shrubs can provide enough shade to attract a mule deer.

Topography. By this we mean the shadow a ridge, hill, butte or mountain might cast as the sun rises or sets. Mule deer will take advantage of that shade as a form of cover, too.

Terrain. Here we're not talking about huge pools of shade like the shadow a butte might produce. Rather, once the sun is up or the day has reached full light, look in any and every bit of shade caused by boulders, rock piles, a slight rise, overhangs, cutbanks, etc. It doesn't take much shade to make a mule deer happy. Note that many of these "micro patches" of shade will be in a draw, gully or wash-out.

To a mule deer, shade is a form of heat relief, security and cover, and you should check out every bit of it.

The shade provided by wash-outs and cut-banks, like these, are prime mule deer bedding spots.

Look Under Your Nose

This is a different concept, but you will be amazed at how many mule deer it will help you find before you spook them out of the country. The idea is this: The grass isn't always greener farther away from you. Start close. Begin looking for mule deer as if the landscape in front of you were a big movie screen. Take a quick look at the entire screen, from the bottom (which is closest to you) up. Look first with the naked eye. If you see anything suspicious, glass it with your binoculars or put the spotting scope on it.

Then commence glassing, starting with the country closest to you, hence the "Under Your Nose" theory. If you glass the hillsides and canyons across the way first, you will sooner or later miss an excellent opportunity immediately in front of or below you. If deer are across the way, there's more than a good chance that you pose no immediate threat; they will hold longer, even if they see you, than one sitting right under your nose.

It's hard to make yourself do this when there's a whole bunch of juicy new country way out there to feast your binoculars on. But starting by looking way off in the distance is a fundamental mistake that will cost you dearly. It has cost the both of us many-a time.

Continued on page 81

Don't miss opportunities under your nose, such as the buck in the bottom of this draw.

Mule Deer Mirage

Mule deer in their natural habitat can be tough to spot. On the pages that follow there are photos of hidden mule deer. Can you find them? Remember "pieces and parts." Keep in mind the images are not always crystal clear in the wild.

One dandy buck, where you'd least expect!

You're still hunting timber, — there's a rump in the trees. If you fail to find it, — another there'll be.

Two nice bucks across the way. Find them soon; I doubt they'll stay.

Two more dandy deer hiding out. Good bucks both, without a doubt.

Another buck, in the brush. Took little time "pegging" us.

Huntin' the brush, you'd best move slow. If they see you first, they're sure to go!

This old buck is trying to hide and let all just walk on by.

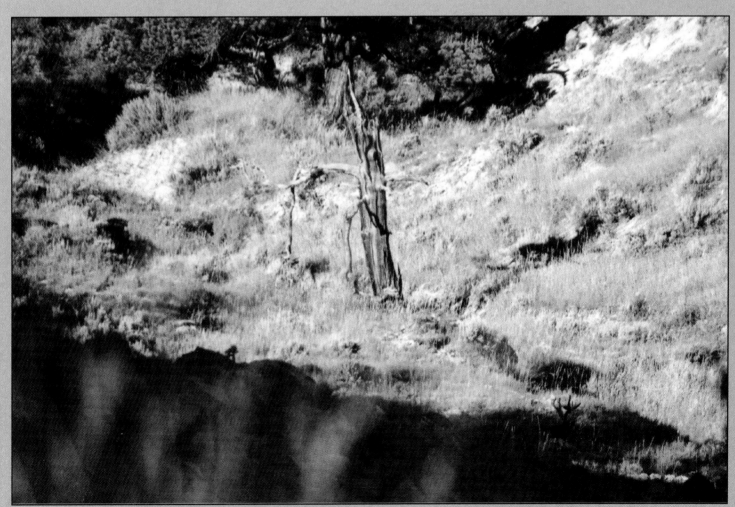

One buck, head on the ground. Has no clue that I'm around.

Thinking we were on a roll, this buck pegged us because we forgot to "scroll".

Here's a couple lyin' low. Hard to find against the snow.

One buck's obvious, and plain to see. The other two take some scrutiny.

This big buck is sleeping sound. Lying flat out, head on the ground

One buck, one doe. Eeny, meeny, miny, mo.

A buck and two mollies, within view. Hidden by now, from only a few.

One nice buck has you made. Remember to keep your eyes on the shade.

A nice young buck, eyes turned away. Make one wrong move and he won't stay.

Mule Deer Gallery

Good solid typical buck in the 175 to 185 class, B&C. Note left eye swelled. A result of the just-completed rut.

Two up-and-coming trophies.

Young buck in the rut.

Note the difference in the ear length on the old buck (right) and the young buck.

Good non-typical buck. This buck was stalked in the '97 bow season by Jim and a hunting client. The photo was taken two months later. Note the ruffed up hair on his upper rib cage where the client's arrow went completely through the buck. This example shows how important razor sharp broad-heads are in the recovery and healing of a buck, hit by a poorly placed shot.

Stopping for a last look.

Grooming perfection.

Snoozin' at dawn.

Getting The Range

To be most effective, concentrate your glassing to an area from fifty yards in front of you out to about two miles away. I've located deer over two miles away with binoculars, but generally they have been up feeding or moving laterally, and the light was just right. Deer are extremely difficult to judge at that distance even with a spotting scope. So I will look only briefly beyond two miles, and that will be just before I get up to move to another location. Even then, most of the time that far-off area I glass will be the area I'm headed for next.

JVN

Find The Sweet Spots

Once you're convinced there is nothing close, glass all the "sweet spots" in the area. Think of sweet spots like this: If you were to hide somewhere in the patch of ground you're looking at, in a place that provided shade a good portion of the morning or evening, offered good camouflage, a great view of approaching danger and a quick escape route, where would you go?

Such places are commonly just below the tops of ridges, under overhangs, at the bottom of cliffs, in rock piles, on any steep and shady north-facing slope providing a view, or in and around pockets of scrub brush, tall grass or sage brush. Also look at the bases of single cedars or junipers, in the midst of scrub cedar patches and in fingers of timber towards the tops of basins and slides.

One factor many of these places have in common is they are out of the wind. What little wind visits these places is often light and variable, affording more opportunities for the deer to scent an intruder. With some experience you'll be able to recognize these likely hideouts with one glance over an area. We've included some photographs that point out examples of these sweet spots. Look at them closely. Try to find similar spots when you are in the field.

This buck has found his own sweet spot— in the shade, just below the crest of a ridge.

Look at all the sweet spots in this patch of country—cut-banks, side draws, overhangs, lone junipers, rockpiles and plenty of shade.

The fingers of timber and slides, above and beyond these pack horses, are good feeding and bedding areas for big mule deer bucks.

Break Up The Country

If you don't find anything in the sweet spots you've identified, break the "movie screen" into narrow corridors 100 to 200 yards wide. Begin looking – in the shade – under cut-banks, near wash-outs, in the gullies and breaks, under overhangs and cliffs, and under scrub cedars, junipers and other conifers. Work your way again from under your nose back to the top of the screen. When you reach the top, start over at the bottom of the next corridor. Methodically scour each corridor, remembering to look for pieces and parts of deer.

Spend extra time looking at isolated areas that appear to have pockets of lush feed. If you see a buck or two, but they're not what you're looking for, keep track of them frequently as you glass. Mule deer bucks often travel in bachelor groups and that big one may be with the group, but just out of sight, perhaps still bedded down or behind a rise.

If you don't locate anything in that sequence, relax for a few minutes. Deer that may be feeding just out of sight could stroll into view, if given a little time. Most mule deer country is filled with more folds, dips and pockets than you can ever hope to see from a single position. Some patient waiting can bring a deer out of one of these features and into plain sight.

After waiting five minutes or so, scan again with the naked eye. Then glass under your nose. Then look at the sweet spots and the corridors again. Repeat the process several times before moving to another location. Glassing the same area from several locations is also a good idea. With each new location you will see the folds, pockets and dips from a different angle; the muleys may be bedded and not moving at the time. Make certain, though, to get to those other locations under cover and out of sight.

Learn Where They Come From

As you discover how mule deer operate and learn their habits and tendencies, you will certainly spook quite a few deer before you see them first. This is to be expected, but don't get discouraged. Instead, spend a considerable amount of time walking up and inspecting their bedding sites and the places they came busting out of. Get an idea of what those places look like, how they are situated in relation to the other terrain, as well as what kind of cover is present and how the deer was using the wind. And as you leave the area, look back at those sites so you have an idea what they look like from a distance.

Keep A Journal

One of the best ways to remember your mule deer hunting experiences is to keep a journal and enter facts and observations for later reference. You'll be surprised at the patterns you begin to note, and then use to your advantage. I've learned in recent years to keep a journal of where I see certain bucks from year to year, what escape routes they use, their favorite bedding sites, and a multitude of other mule deer facts that will help my limited memory. It's a great habit to get into from the start. What took me thirty-three years to perfect might only take you five!

JVN

Out-of-the-Way Spots

Once older, more experienced mule deer bucks notice a little pressure, they generally retreat to the roughest, toughest country in the area. High-mountain monarchs will generally retreat into the dark timber and stay there. Some bucks use a different strategy and completely vacate the rough stuff. They instead hide out in the lower elevations where they find spots which look totally unlike deer country. These unlikely areas offer the least disturbed, most secluded hideouts around.

Bucks using either strategy have a tendency to go nocturnal, arriving in their feeding areas at dark and leaving before daylight, if venturing out in the open at all. This requires you to glass the sweet spots and heavy cover dili-gently before the sun rises, and after it sets until dark.

The bottom line here: You can probably find some mule deer in the classic terrain. But if you're hunting a general season or other hunting slot where pressure is noticeable or even heavy, go where no one else goes to find big bucks. Even if the area doesn't look like much. This might mean bivouacking out at timberline, or working the big sage miles from any mountain or hill.

Ignore the beaten path to find mule deer bucks that grow old ... and sport racks like this.

Read The Habitat

If you're hunting an area you're unfamiliar with and haven't had an opportunity to scout – scouting should be done long before the season opens, by the way – here's a tip that could simplify your decisions on where to look for mule deer.

Learn to read the habitat and landscape for mule deer. It's like learning to read the water while fishing, and it's an essential part of being successful at either endeavor.

To compare finding mule deer with fishing, consider the sun and the wind to be water flowing over the terrain. Where would you find the eddies, holes, backwaters and resting places for a fish? By using the same train of thought for muleys – with the holes and resting places being shade and shelter, the eddies and backwaters being where little wind and disturbance exists – you will begin to understand where to start.

Big fish lay where they can catch food that's being carried downstream. Big mule deer lay where their noses can catch scent – flowing downwind – and keep themselves from becoming food! Similarly, a large fish will lie in a position where the territory he is occupying can easily be monitored. So do big muleys.

Use the wind and sun as two separate stream flows in your evaluation. That is – the suns rays will be coming from one direction, the wind will generally be coming from another; but the combination creates a sweet spot where the deer is under cover and can see things he can't smell and can smell things coming from where he can't see.

With some experience, finding mule deer in their habitat is like becoming a speed reader. Upon first gaze you'll read the country, then note the sweet spots and pick out the important subject matter, being sure to read all the footnotes if the sweet spots don't pan out.

When To Look

Like most other game, you're more likely to spot mule deer out and about and on the move at dawn and dusk. This is, of course, an excellent time to glass because the deer will certainly be easier to spot. Plus, their movement is more likely to bring them out of those landscape dips and folds, and into your corridor of vision as you wait and look.

On the other hand, don't waste mid-day hours napping or trudging back to camp for lunch. Stay out and hunt! From a stalking standpoint, 10 a.m. to 2 p.m. on a warm day is a great time to stalk mule deer. Although they're bedded and harder to spot than when up and moving, they are almost always stationary, sometimes a bit sleepy and will likely remain so for awhile. That combination often presents some good stalking opportunities.

It also helps that the winds are usually a bit more predictable at midday. And the thermal currents should be subsiding from their morning rise and not yet starting their evening descent as the air cools.

Between 11:00 a.m. and 2:00 p.m., you can also see some mule deer up and moving. Generally they are changing bedding sites as their shade diminishes.

Leave No Stone Unturned

No matter where or when you're looking, be thorough. Mule deer bucks can be in the oddest, most out-of-the-way places; places you wouldn't think to look. And that's exactly why they go there. So looking in the classic spots is fine, but also slow down to look at that weird boulder over there, that rockpile out in the middle of nowhere, that stunted little juniper standing all alone on that steep slope, or that cut bank way down in the bottom of the gully. I've seen mule deer in all these places. Mule deer are predictable to a point; but in the end they are where you find them.

TJC

Notice the buck bedded in the shade of the lone scrub cedar (lower right).

Chapter 6

Seeing the Gray Ghost—How to Look

Introduction

We're building, step-by-step, the skills for a successful spot-and-stalk strategy for hunting mule deer. So far, you've learned about mule deer and their habits, seen the exact pieces and parts you should be looking for when trying to spot mule deer, and gotten advice on where to look to find these pieces and parts.

But the lesson isn't complete yet. No matter how good your eyes are, or how good you are at picking out sweet spots and knowing where to look, there is one more critical element to locating mule deer you'll need to know before you begin the actual stalk. That is how to go about looking for mule deer.

The reason this is so critical is simple. You have to locate the deer, which in many cases translates into getting into position to locate the deer, without them seeing or smelling you, or knowing in any way that you are there. You

have to have a strategy and plan in place before going out to glass for mule deer. There's much more to looking for mule deer than just wandering around the countryside and glassing a few hillsides here and there, or plopping yourself down on a ridge in broad view of everything for miles and hoping to spot an animal that's not already decided to leave the area.

The knowledge in this chapter will help you quietly and secretively get around the countryside to spot mule deer before they spot you. We'll start with some advice on your most important spotting tool. Other than your own eyes and a healthy dose of patience, optics are of prime importance. Then we'll describe, in detail, strategies and techniques for getting your eyes and optics into position to find a calm mule deer going about his business.

OPTICS

Since top-notch optics are one of the keys to mule deer hunting success, the best rule of thumb is this: Always buy optics one notch above what you can afford. You will never, ever be sorry. Your spouse may "biff" you with them when you get home from the store or af-

ter they arrive from the cataloger, but it will be worth it in the long run, guaranteed. And since you might get biffed with them, if they're good-quality gear they are less likely to be damaged when they hit you.

Essential tools of the hunt: good binoculars, spotting scope, portable tripod, truck window mount for spotting scope.

Making A Living Behind Optics

Having guided mule deer hunters for many years, I guess I've seen about every type and brand of binocular made and many of the spotting scopes as well. I've tried dozens of variations myself, and always noted what was being carried by my clients and how efficient they were with the equipment.

There are a few rules to follow. The number one consideration, in my book, is to strive for minimum eye fatigue. Glassing all day, every day, for several weeks during the hunting season, and almost every other day of the year, to boot (albeit in smaller chunks) has taught me some hard lessons. These lessons have been paid for with major eye strain or whopper headaches.

JVN

Binoculars

When choosing binoculars stay between seven and eight power. Seven by thirty-five (7 X 35), eight by thirty (8 X 30) or eight by forty-two's (8 X 42) are all excellent choices. Ten power (10X) is probably too much magnification. There is no way to hold such big lenses completely still for an entire day, let alone several days of hard hunting. Plus, most 10X binoculars are very bulky and heavy, making carrying them great distances out of the question. If they are not too heavy, they are so light you have to hold your breath to steady them. You'll not only pay more for 10X's in dollars, but you'll also pay more in eye fatigue. And that will take enjoyment away from your hunt.

Try to get binoculars with individual eye focus – the kind you can set to your own eyes and leave there. Mark the settings with a fine-point felt marker, then look at the settings each time before pulling them up to your eyes, making certain the glass is focused on your settings and ready to go. This will save you time otherwise wasted as you adjust back and forth, not to mention the eyestrain you'll avoid.

Rolling a single, center focus ring back and forth to get a clear picture, each time you glass, can be hard on your eyes. Most of these types of binoculars allow you to set the focus on one eye, with the focus ring taking care of the other eye. But invariably while hunting on foot or horseback or riding in a truck, the focus ring shifts. To reduce eyestrain, if you have one of these types, mark the center focus ring where the glass is in focus at about 100 yards. Set it there before you pull them up to your eyes, allowing you then to make only small focus adjustments. You should be able to minimize eye fatigue.

A Place For 10-Powers

If you have 10X binoculars, don't despair. I carry a pair of 10X Steiners (a gift from a relative) in the truck, and I only use them there – leaning them against the door or resting them on the window when looking. Even then, I use them sparingly as they're still hard to steady and I can't afford the headaches. Use your 10X's in similar ways, and get some good 7X's or 8X's for the field.

JVN

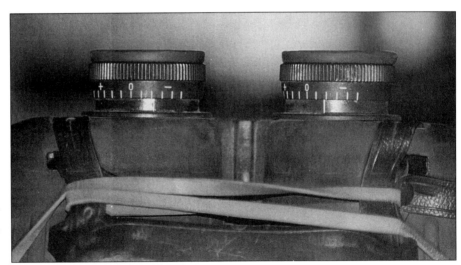

Binoculars with individual-eye focus.

Tips On Using Binoculars

You'll be amazed at how much time you spend behind a prism in mule deer country. The landscape is always so vast, you have to use your binoculars constantly and effectively. In addition to getting quality optics, you have to know how to use them. This includes learning to keep the binoculars steady to reduce eyestrain, and learning how to sight quickly and easily on something you've noticed first with your naked eyes. Here are some tips from someone who has spent many-a day behind binoculars over the last couple decades.

If you're huffing and puffing from a climb or from moving fast to get into position, take a moment to calm down. You need to do this if you are preparing to shoot your rifle or draw your bow, and you should do it with binoculars in hand as well. Slower breathing will keep those glasses steady, reducing wear-and-tear on your eyes. In addition, you'll be able to key directly onto the subject easier.

Sit on your rump and steady your elbows on your knees as you peer through the binoculars. This is simple but effective, as is resting the glasses over a rock or downed tree, if available. You can even lean up against a tree trunk to make everything more still.

If nothing is handy to steady your viewing, try this. Rest the binoculars on your thumbs, then use your index fingers as braces against your temples. It works.

If you see something interesting with your naked eyes, don't look down to your binoculars, grab them and scan to relocate it. Instead, stare at the spot, and bring your binoculars slowly up to your eyes. Don't move your head or shift your eyes. You should then be right on target.

Binoculars are great, but respect them. They are powerful, and these few simple rules can save your eyes and eliminate headaches. These tips are worth the extra time they take.

TJC

Sit on your rump and rest your elbows on your knees.

Use anything and everything available — even the ground — to steady your binoculars.

Spotting Scopes

Spotting scope power is also over emphasized. A twenty power (20X) scope is all you really need for mule deer, elk or antelope hunting in the west. Anything over 20X becomes a detriment once the heat waves come into play. The mirage plays havoc with what you're looking at, and you just won't get a clear image. Don't buy a variable-power spotting scope; you will work your eyes too hard zooming back and forth.

If you have a variable-power scope already, don't look through it as you zoom. Zoom first, then look. Also, as you get up to the higher powers, clarity suffers greatly. For the money spent, a straight 20X spotting scope will serve you the best. Don't worry if you feel a little under-glassed; you're not. If you can't quite count all the points on a buck, get a little closer. Think of it this way; the more eye strain you punish yourself with, the more chance you have of missing that Boone and Crockett antler sticking out of the buck brush. We'll take lower power and more good hours in the field any day! (That goes for binoculars too.)

A portable tripod will steady your view through a spotting scope.

General Advice – Clarity And Light, Waterproof, Armor

Whether it's binoculars or spotting scopes, look for equipment that is clear and bright, is waterproof, and is tough and durable.

Consider clarity and light-gathering capabilities first. Most companies these days are striving for more clarity in their binoculars and spotting scopes. It's getting to the point where it is harder to tell the difference in clarity, until you get into the very, very expensive models. In any case,

make sure the images you see are bright and sharp, right to the very edges of the field of view. Stay away from glass that is noticeably clearer in the middle of the field of view, then becomes fuzzy towards the outer edges.

Light-gathering capability for low light situations is very important for early-morning and late-evening hunting, the prime times to be out and looking. You will never get the light gathering capabilities or the brightness you need from the smaller objective (front) lenses. Binoculars with 30mm to 42mm objective lenses are nowhere near as good at gathering light as those with 50mm or 56mm lenses. Also remember there can be a real difference in brightness and light gathering capabilities between lenses of the same size. Simply look at a distance ceiling light in the sporting goods store, when trying various binoculars or spotting scopes (making certain you are comparing identical powers) and note the difference in brightness.

Next – and this is very important – only buy binoculars and spotting scopes that are waterproof. Not water-resistant. Waterproof. There's nothing worse than finally getting up a

mountain to that special spot only to have your spotting equipment fog up, forcing you to make due with your naked eyes because a little mist or snow is falling. Make certain that what you buy is guaranteed waterproof. Mule deer country is often dry; but don't count on it. The weather can be brutally wet, foggy and cold for days on end.

Finally, binoculars and spotting scopes must be rubber-armored. No matter how careful you are, you're going to drop them, drag them across some rocks while stalking on your belly, flop them out of the truck, the horse will step on them – you get the idea. The rubber-armored types just endure the abuse better.

HOW TO FIND MULE DEER

So, now you know what you're looking for, and where you should be looking to see those mule deer pieces and parts. With good optics in hand and a huge chunk of real estate in front of you, it's time to get to work moving around and looking for mule deer. How do you go about it?

Here are strategies and tactics that will help

you find mule deer long before they find you. The tips here will also help in every aspect of your overall mule deer hunting efforts.

But remember. The main idea behind what's described here is to give you specific techniques you can use to find mule deer without mule deer finding you first.

Scrolling

While hunting, or while moving from one bit of country to another to get to a likely glassing spot, never skyline yourself. Most hunters know this, but it's worth repeating and thinking about at all times while in the field. Skylining yourself is a sure way to warn every mule deer in the drainage of your presence.

That said, it's interesting that few hunters know how to "scroll" up small portions of territory, when they start looking over the top of a rise of any type. So, our careful hunter, working hard to walk below the crest of a ridge instead of up-top where it's easier,

might suddenly climb up to a vantage point where he or she can see an entire piece of new country and then begin glassing it. This could work – and sometimes it does – if it can be accomplished under cover. But a great majority of the time, even if you have some cover, it just won't work.

Unless you "scroll" the new country into view, any mule deer in that area will have you pegged as your out-of-place silhouette clambers around on the horizon. The scrolling method eliminates this problem. Here's how to do it.

Skylining yourself, from a buck's perspective. He won't stick around.

Scrolling will present opportunities like this.

How To Scroll

As you come to the crest of a ridge, hill, canyon, rise (any kind of elevation or terrain you want to see over), just as soon as you can see <u>any</u> portion of the country beyond the crest, stop and take a quick look with the naked eye, then begin glassing. Use the crest line of the terrain as your "underscore" line, the line hiding most of your body from view.

Glass the landscape above the line thoroughly. Again, look for small portions of the deer as opposed to the whole animal. Then move forward ever so slightly and begin the process of looking with the naked eye and then glassing once again. In effect you are scrolling up the next piece of territory lying directly below the first.

Do this from your belly, knees or on your feet, whatever you feel is warranted for the situation. If you elect to stay on your feet, make certain you have a backdrop of some sort to prevent skylining and remember to move very slowly. That's worth repeating – move very slowly. While on our feet, we all have a tendency to move too hastily; moving too quickly and barging over the hill is precisely what can get you into trouble.

By scrolling up small portions of country at a time, you'll soon begin to spot little pieces of what you're looking for long before they see you. This method also affords you the opportunity to then back off and stalk into position for a better look, if you see something you like – such as the antlers of a nice buck that has no idea you're there. You'll also be in a position to carefully plan an effective stalk, or maybe even come back over for your shot if you're hunting with a rifle and the deer is close enough.

Scrolling will help you spot a buck like this before he sees you. Note how the terrain hides you from the deer.

A Scrolling Tip

If there are places that are out of your field of view as you scroll up some country, and you think they could be good spots for muleys, back up below the horizon and move laterally 50 yards or so. Then start your scrolling process again from a different angle. Repeat this process as necessary to get a look into all the pockets of cover.

It all boils down to taking your time and being thorough. I'm fairly upset with myself after I stumble up to a spot, plop down to glass and all I see is a big rack, swaying back and forth, headed for the tall timber. Scrolling is the solution, and just a little patience and extra effort will provide great opportunities!

JVN

Scrolling: THE Key Concept

Until you see the scrolling technique in use, you can't really appreciate its effectiveness. I never really thought about it until I saw Jim do it.

The first time we hunted together and I watched him scroll up a piece of country, I didn't understand the concept. It seemed to be taking an awfully long time to look over the other side of the finger gully we were hunting as he inched his way up the hillside, step by slow step, leaning forward and peering over the top edge as the new country came into view across and below.

But then he slowly backed down, motioned me forward, showed me where to look, and there was a muley buck, not more than 30 yards away, oblivious to our presence. I watched the deer flick a few flies, nod his head a few drowsy times, test the wind, look here and there and just do what mule deer bucks generally do all day.

It was incredible to watch, at such close range, a deer go about his business. We elected not to try to get the extra few yards into bow range as our hunt was only a few hours old and there was sure to be some bigger bucks around. So we backed down, dusted ourselves off and went looking for another buck.

That was the moment I dropped out of the school of barge, plop and look and graduated to the college of scrolling!

TJC

Skirting Strategy

In much of the West, the country is rough and broken up with a series of main ridges running between drainages, a series of "hogbacks" running perpendicular to the ridges, then wash-outs and draws that lead down into the drainages. The topography will vary, but the common denominator is this: The country is steep and rough and not easy for two-legged hunters to navigate. These types of areas are prime mule deer habitat.

Similarly, areas of rolling sand hills with blowouts, wash-outs and tall sagebrush should not be overlooked as prime habitat, even though these spots look even less romantic than their high-country counterparts.

When hunting a main ridge in either type of area, don't walk down the top; that skylines you from both sides. But then you have to make a decision on which side of the ridge to hunt and which side to "skirt." Skirting means to travel along the ridge laterally, just below the ridge line and out of sight of the primary side you want to hunt.

The number one consideration here, of course, is the wind direction. If you're an experienced hunter, you know the rule. If you're just starting out hunting or haven't really worried much about wind before, the idea is this: Make certain your scent is blowing away from where you think the deer are. The second consideration is which side of the ridge contains the most shade. As discussed before, finding the shade is key to finding mule deer. Consequently mule deer bucks seem to prefer slopes facing north, but steep slopes facing west are also excellent as they provide shade a good portion of the day. In the best of all hunting worlds, the two considerations will work together for you, with the wind blowing from the shade to you.

In this case, let's say, you've chosen to hunt the west side of the ridge and skirt the east side. Before proceeding, thoroughly glass the areas ahead and east of you – the ones you're totally exposed to – making certain there's not something standing in the open, being extremely obvious.

Now proceed along the east side, just below the ridge crest, stopping every 100 to 200 yards to peek over to the west side using the scrolling method we've already discussed. It's best to scroll on your stomach, so as not to sky-line yourself any more than absolutely necessary. As an option, stay on your knees or at the least, crouch. Don't stand straight up, because your profile will draw immediate and undivided attention.

Thoroughly glass narrow corridors 100 to 200 yards wide within your scope of view. If you determine nothing is within view, back up below the crest again (out of sight of the west side) and proceed down the east side of the ridge another 100 to 200 yards. Then scroll into the west side again. Repeat this sequence as you slowly work your way along.

When possible, always take a second look at the previous corridors, as you'll now be looking at them from a different angle. This is very important, with all the dips, folds, pockets and wash-outs that dominate the landscape.

Every other corridor or so, you should stop, sit down and glass the drainage and slopes east of you (again, the ones you're totally exposed to). If you spot a deer over there, he probably sees you by now. If he's the one you're looking for, try the "Beg Your Pardon Retreat" described later on.

Skirting, scrolling and glassing corridors seems like a lot of work, and it is. But it is hunting in the truest sense of the word; it is fun; and it will make the difference between wondering where the deer are, and successfully finding mule deer before they see you first.

As you skirt your way along a ridge, remember to scroll as you take new looks at the country. It's the only way to assure that every deer in the drainage won't spot you.

Mr. No Shoulders

One caution here. When on your stomach, always keep an eye out for "Mr. No Shoulders" (rattlesnake) as he has been known to be crabby when met face-to-face at ground level. He normally won't hurt you, only warn you. But he could make you hurt yourself as you abandon that particular scrolling sequence!

JVN

The "Beg Your Pardon Retreat"

Sometimes – and this happens to all of us – we're not as good as we thought at skirting and scrolling. No matter how careful you think you are, when you top that little rise or bring your binoculars up to your eyes, there's your buck, lying in the shade, staring right at you. "Holy cow muffin, what to do now!"

There is a tactic that has worked very well over the years, putting more than its share of mature mule deer bucks on the meat pole.

Slowly get up, turn, and go back the way you came. Don't crouch or sneak, just calmly and nonchalantly walk away. Deer can see your body language, and they know a skulking predator when they see one. In short, your objective is to get out of sight as soon as you can, but also as slowly and calmly as is practical.

Now it depends on how long you've been there, as to whether the deer will leave once you're out of sight. Old mature bucks will generally leave if you've been there any length of time or were extremely close. Regardless, once you are out of the deer's line of sight, move laterally 40 to 50 yards either way, and sneak back into position, preferably on your belly and under cover, for another look. Don't waste too much time getting into position, as big bucks have a definite tendency to leave.

It is very important to determine if the buck was really spooked, or is simply sneaking away. Mule deer bucks are fat and fairly lazy, especially in the early fall, and if simply sneaking away may bed back down within a reasonably short distance. Many times you can keep them in view all the way to their new bedding site. But be careful because nine times out of 10, he will be lying and looking back where he first saw you, contemplating where you went and wondering if you're coming back!

If the deer is still there, and the majority of the time he will be, wait for him to settle down considerably before attempting a stalk or preparing for a shot. Indications of a calm deer could include: turning his attention away from the spot where you disappeared; relaxing his ears; shaking his ears, head or tail; or extending a leg to move into a more comfortable position.

When a deer is still in his original position, even though you thought he surely would have left, use caution as you try to work into a good position. He's probably hanging around because there are more deer in the area.

The "I Give Up" Tactic

After glassing an entire area and seemingly exhausting all the possibilities without spotting a deer, stand up in full view. Walk out into the open and move laterally, either way, 20 yards or so and take a seat. If you've missed a bedded or hidden buck, he definitely sees you now. Mule deer are very patient if they think you don't see them. Big bucks will freeze for long periods hoping you will leave.

Wait a full 10 to 15 minutes, not using your glasses or spotting scope, so your naked eye can pick up any movement within view. When the deer sees you're not going anywhere, he will finally get nervous and move out.

This strategy confirms one of several things. First, it can tell you there are no deer within your scope of view. Second, it may present an opportunity for a shot if you're rifle hunting. Mule deer sometimes stop for one last look as they leave the area. Third, this strategy may give you the opportunity to find the deer after he picks another bedding site. As mentioned before, mule deer bucks are fat and fairly lazy and will usually lie back down in a short period of time, if not spooked too badly.

Always Look for a Crowd

Except during the rut or in the case of really smart, old loners (ridge runners as my father used to call them), mule deer bucks seldom travel alone. Bachelor groups average 2 to 7 in size and travel together during the summer and fall months. I've seen up to 15 in one group.

So, whenever you spot a buck that seems to be alone, spend plenty of time glassing the vicinity for more deer. If you locate nothing else, back off and move laterally to glass from another location and get a new view of the area. That's often when you'll see the pieces and parts of other deer.

I always assume there are other deer in hiding. Work to locate them, as they take great pleasure in blowing your stalk and then watching you stomp your equipment in despair.

JVN

Summer bachelor group of bucks.

When you see one mule deer, look for others; if you don't, the ones you don't see will bust your stalk. This group has paused in its escape, to look back. But don't shoot the broken-horned buck— there's a doe behind him!

Conclusion

Use the strategies and tactics outlined here to move around in mule deer country and see the deer before they see you. You'll then be ready to plan and execute your stalk to get into surefire range of your bow, muzzleloader or rifle.

Chapter 7

Stalking

Introduction

Up to now, everything in this book has focused on getting you in position to spot a calm buck so you can plan a stalk. Spotting and stalking is the true essence of mule deer hunting, and the method works in all the muley habitat types. No matter where you're hunting, stalking a deer you've spotted is an exciting challenge. If you do it successfully, it is also quite an accomplishment.

Now if you're good at sneaking around the countryside and spotting mule deer, you'll be surprised at how close you can sometimes get before you see the animals. In fact, if you're hunting with a centerfire rifle you may not need to stalk at all because you might already be within a couple hundred yards of your quarry.

But sooner or later, even with a rifle in hand, you'll need to get closer to the deer or into a better position to get a good, sure shot. If you're hunting with muzzleloader or bow, you'll almost certainly

Yes, you CAN get close enough, even with archery equipment, to get muley bucks like this.

need to pull off a stalk once the deer is spotted.

Now we realize that many hunters don't have much opportunity to practice stalking. Their normal hunting grounds are heavily wooded and require stand hunting and deer drives to get bucks. If you are one of these hunters, probably a dyed-in-the-wool white-tail fanatic, this chapter will open another facet of hunting to you, a facet you must experience to believe. If you already hunt and stalk mule deer, you're sure to pick up plenty of new insights and pointers here.

Stalking is exciting and nerve-racking. At times it is frustrating and disappointing. But the rewards of a successful stalk outweigh all other methods of hunting, guaranteed. Besides, stalking is a very effective way to take mule deer bucks and, if done properly, will produce awesome results – results you might not think possible.

The biggest bucks are, as usual, harder to take. But by choosing your stalks carefully and following a few basic rules, you can get close enough for an excellent rifle shot. Even with a bow-and-arrow in hand, an up-close and personal chance at the buck of a lifetime is a real possibility!

When To Stalk

Generally, 10:00 a.m. to 2:00 p.m. on a warm day is the best time for stalking mule deer. The bucks are almost always in the shade, they're stationary, and sometimes sleepy. Many hunters miss this opportune time to pursue mule deer because they've decided to wait until the deer start moving again near the end of the day. And, some hunters just want to dodge the warmth themselves, or take their own mid-day siesta.

Early mornings and evenings lend themselves better to glassing and then getting ahead of traveling deer, or waiting for a buck at water or along trails that lead to and from feeding areas. Evening stalks often end in darkness, short

of your destination. For the most part, late-morning to mid-afternoon presents the best opportunities for stalking.

The Stalking Arena

Some country lends itself better to stalking than other areas. Most mule deer country has two types of opportunities within the same area. The first is the hard-to-stalk type: heavy brush, black timber or wide open, rolling hills. Then there is the easier-to-stalk type: canyons, draws, cut-banks, wash-outs, etc. All these areas offer shade and limited vegetation. Notice we said these areas are "easier" to stalk not "easy."

A mule deer's senses are so acute, successful stalking in heavy vegetation is tough, sometimes impossible. The same goes for

Gaining Stalking Experience

My viewpoint on experience is this: Experience is a wonderful thing; it enables you to recognize a mistake when you make it again!

Stalking takes practice. So if you're new to the game take a little time while in the field and sneak up on some does or small bucks you don't want to shoot. It's great fun and you'll learn more with each attempt. This is knowledge you can use when a big buck appears in your binoculars or spotting scope.

Trial and error over the years is what ultimately cultivates a stalking expert. So our goal here is to help you eliminate years of experience (mistakes) and become a more successful stalker in a shorter period of time.

JVN

open, rolling hills. At best, both are low-percentage endeavors. Stalking can be done, but it requires extreme patience and a flawless approach.

On the other hand, rough, cut-up and sparsely vegetated country presents more opportunities to approach unnoticed. This is because shade (the number one place to find mule deer bucks) is a limited commodity here. It is found only under cut-banks, washouts, overhangs, etc. and under the limited vegetation.

So if you're planning to stalk, especially with archery equipment, pick an area that will present the high-percentage opportunities. As we will discuss, picking only high-percentage stalks is one of the keys to being a top-notch stalker.

Clothing And Boots For Stalking

The selection of proper boots and clothing is one of the most important, yet commonly overlooked, factors of successful stalking. Probably a third of all blown stalks are caused by noise from boots or clothing. Here are some guidelines for decreasing the noise and improving your chances.

Boots. Choose boots with a lot of support, but soft to medium soles. The popular "waffle-stomper" sole is a poor choice. Its radical configuration has a tendency to be very hard. Such soles will break and crackle dry foliage. Additionally, this type of boot can "clack" on rocks and is extremely noisy crunching on dry earth. Instead, choose a sole that has some flexibility. Try a soft, rubbery sole with no traction bars. The sole should provide good traction with little or no slippage, and mold around things you step on rather than grind them into the ground. A boot that is water proof is almost a must. Dew can be heavy at times on some fall mornings. Today's Gore-Tex lined models are perfect. Plain rubber boots are also great for

stalking, if you can stand the heat. A removable lining that can be easily dried out is very important with a rubber boot because you'll sweat it up as you work your way around mule deer country.

Outer Clothes. Wool is hard to beat as an outer layer because it makes very little noise. Fleece outer garments and pants are also excellent choices. Avoid anything that is nylon or a nylon blend. It will invariably be too noisy. Avoid heavy canvas types of outer garments as well. Pick your head gear and gloves with the same criteria in mind. Finding quiet rain gear is very important too, as some of the best stalking weather is while it's raining or snowing. Keep in mind that layering your clothing is important in mule deer country. You'll have periods of exertion and inactivity alternating all day. So give some thought to your under layers and their noise production because you may end up stalking without your usual outer layer on.

Getting Into Position

Although the best opportunities for stalking occur when the sun has been up for several hours, it's important to be out and in position before daylight. Have a position determined, before opening day, that will provide a panoramic view of a lot of country. This position should be well-hidden and off the skyline. It can be in a rockpile, on the edge of some brush, against a tree or any place that will break up your silhouette. It should also be in a place where you're not limited to glassing directly into the sun as it rises.

Approaching your vantage point in the dark, make certain you are obscured from view by the terrain as much as possible. Use your flashlight sparingly, and only point it at the ground. The only time you should be visible to the country you're planning to glass is when you "top over" the skyline to get into glassing position.

If no cover is available as you cross over, make the transition quickly and get under the ridge line as soon as practical and take a seat. If you had to use a flashlight to get up there, turn it off before you top over. If the cover is sparse, there's more than a good chance that a mule deer may pick up the movement, but sometimes it's a chance you'll have to take.

Once in position remain as motionless as possible until it gets light enough to begin glassing. If a deer did pick up your movement as you topped over, he might be reassured if there's no further movement. When it gets light, move sparingly and slowly while panning the landscape.

Another option is to remain hidden on the other side of the ridge. Don't top over in the dark; rather, use the scrolling method to look into your planned glassing area when it's light enough.

Either of these methods will give you opportunities to observe more mule deer while they're out feeding, and possibly find the one you're looking for. You might find several bucks you would like to have a crack at. These tactics will allow you to observe the deer until they pick a bedding site, then you can evaluate which stalk affords the best opportunity.

Although waiting for a deer to bed while rifle hunting is not quite as critical as it is while bowhunting, it's still a good idea if there's not too much other hunting competition around. The deer is then stationary and you are generally not guessing where he went when you arrive near his last location.

THREE KEY CONSIDERATIONS

Once you've located the mule deer you want there are three main considerations in beginning a successful stalk. First, evaluate the overall opportunity. Given the deer's position, your position and the cover (vegetative or topographical) available to help you, what are your chances of getting where you need to be? Second, consider wind direction. Can you get there without the wind carrying your scent to the deer? Third, mentally map your stalking route. Is it a plan you can remember and follow?

Evaluate The Overall Opportunity

Is this an excellent, good, mediocre or poor stalking opportunity? Many stalks are blown because they were mediocre or poor opportunities to begin with. This is especially true in bowhunting, but don't underestimate this factor for rifle hunting. The fewer blown stalks, the less chance you have of running your buck completely out of the country.

Don't stalk unless you think you have a good or excellent chance. It's not worth trying to turn a mediocre or poor opportunity into something it's not, especially if it's a buck dreams are made of. If you're a diligent hunter, be patient. There will be another opportunity at that buck another day, or maybe even this day if he's worth waiting around for and watching for a few hours. (If you're that excited about him, he may well be worth watching all day until that stalking opportunity comes up.) Besides, having to lie and watch a big buck positioned where there's no approach to him builds hunting character. You'll acquire more respect for the deer. That respect will be part of what makes you more effective when you finally get a chance to move out after him.

When bowhunting, your evaluation needs to be even more in-depth. Ask yourself, "Can I get into position for a responsible shot?" And then ask, "Can I draw without being seen when he stands up?" Also ask, "If I have to wait a while for the deer to stand and offer a shot, is the wind dependable?" What's the terrain and footing going to be like as you get critically close to the deer?

Although stalking tactics for rifle hunting are not quite as detailed, you should carefully evaluate them. Are there other deer and are they going to spook or wind you before you get in position. Will they alert your objective deer? Once you go around the other deer, can you still get a clear shot or would it be wise to wait for a better opportunity?

Evaluate The Wind

Next, evaluate the wind, asking yourself these questions: "Is the wind variable or steady? Is it variable to the point that a stalk seems folly, or is it acting steady enough that I might be able to trust it to continue carrying my scent away from the deer? Can I approach the deer with the wind directly in my face, or at the very least will it be a quartering or cross wind? Considering that wind, where is my best stalking route? Is the wind blowing hard enough to cover some of my noisy mistakes?"

Mule deer bucks test the breeze often, and rely on what it tells them.

Don't hesitate to stalk in a very stiff wind. Many people are annoyed by strong wind, and so are the animals. But take advantage of this great opportunity to stalk mule deer. It's true that big bucks are very nervous during periods of strong wind, but they also have a tendency to hold better when an inadvertent noise is made during a big blow. They are very alert as always, but often perceive the slip of a stalker's step or the snap of a twig as caused by the wind. The wind, of course, also hides many other noises such as shoe squeaks, brushes of fabric against foliage, camera shutters, a rifle safety clicking and arrow nocks snapping onto strings. All those last-second, noisy details may be missed by the acute mule deer ears when the wind is up.

A good, strong wind from one direction simply eliminates much of the guesswork involved with working in an unpredictable, variable wind. In fact, a variable wind ruins more stalks than any other detail of the hunt. That fickle, ever-changing breeze will sooner or later swirl your scent to the deer and you'll wind up sneaking to an empty bed. Evaluating wind properly is key to selecting the right stalking opportunity.

Map Your Stalk

Mapping your stalk mentally is the remaining critical planning element. The key here is to plan a route containing three solid check points that you can easily recognize as you close in on the deer. These should be prominent landmarks that are not easily mistaken. If you fail to do this, you may well find yourself in the wrong place as the buck bolts away.

It's always surprising how different the country looks when you start sneaking through it, as opposed to the view from where you glassed. That's why the three prominent checkpoints are critical to your stalk's success. Pick out a dead tree, an unusually shaped stump or snag, distinctively colored or shaped boulders, certain rock piles or outcroppings, a specific cut-bank, any feature with unique details will work. Avoid using objects that are excessively common and could be confusing.

Three Checkpoints On The Map

Although the actual location of the deer deserves a strong mental note, your third checkpoint should be where you want to attempt a shot from if rifle or muzzle-loader hunting. While bowhunting, you'll wait at the third checkpoint for an opportunity for a shot. The second checkpoint should be about halfway to the third point and should be at a location where you can, without being seen, confirm checkpoint number three and see if the deer is still there. The first checkpoint should be something that confirms, after leaving your glassing site and proceeding toward your objective, that you have ended up in the right draw, drainage or gully to begin your stalk.

Notice we worked backwards in determining checkpoints. The number three checkpoint should be foremost in your mind. Engrave it on your brain because this is your ultimate goal. Knowing this final checkpoint is critical because if you happen to miss number two, you still have some idea where you're going.

Use The Terrain

When selecting your route between checkpoints, use the terrain as much as possible to hide your movements from the deer's view. Don't depend on bushes or trees to hide you as you approach. A muley's peripheral vision is wonderfully acute and will serve him well unless your approach is totally obscured by topographical features.

If you can't stalk totally obscured by the terrain, maybe you need to wait for a better opportunity.

Partners And Hand Signals

When stalking, it really helps to have a series of hand signals worked out. Leave your hunting partner back where you spotted the deer. The signals should help direct you as you're stalking. They should also tell you the status of the deer (alert, calm, standing and looking, on the move, gone). Keep the hand signals very simple, and use them as confirmation or information, not as your primary guide. Your selected checkpoints are your guides to the deer.

Two Tips: Think "Shade" And "Other Deer"

Use shade to your advantage as much as possible while stalking. Camouflage patterns and movement are much harder for deer to pick up in the shadows.

And, when stalking mule deer, always assume there are other deer you didn't see hiding in the area. If you don't figure them into the equation, they will almost certainly end up somewhere along the path to one of your checkpoints. These animals take great pleasure in blowing your stalk.

COMPLETING THE STALK

Treading Carefully: Foot Placement

While stalking, foot placement is very important. Keep your feet farther apart than normal, so your pant legs won't "swish." Avoid any broadleaf plants or seed pods; seed pods become dry in the fall and rattle when brushed. Also, remember that most plants have dead foliage from the previous year among their green foliage. Something you think won't make any noise can surprise you. So just avoid as many plants as possible. When that's not possible, slow your pace down. Take a few steps and stop for at least 30 seconds. Take a few more, stop again and so on.

If you make a mistake by stepping on something extremely noisy, stop for five minutes. If the buck heard you, he will pay attention to the location of the sound until he's sure there's nothing to be afraid of. You could try pausing for less time, but a five-minute delay should definitely reassure him. The noise made by birds, mice, chipmunks, squirrels, gophers and other animals, as well as falling rocks, sliding dirt, dry leaves falling from trees and other non-animal sounds, are all normal parts of a mule deer's day. They will check out odd noises and listen for a while, then go back to what they were doing.

Occasionally one of these critters will give you a warning signal as you invade it's territory – a pika will bark or a chipmunk or squirrel will start chattering. You know how it goes. Pay attention to these sounds and wait your allotted five minutes if you hear one of these warnings. You have to wait because that mule deer buck will be listening, too. If the varmint continuously scolds you, stop and wait until things settle down.

Take Some Rests

Stalking, especially during a bow hunt, is very physically demanding. It's important to be

in good shape, and even if you're in top condition, take time at the first two checkpoints to rest and extend your legs. Taking slow deliberate steps is very taxing on leg muscles, and you don't want to get to checkpoint number three and have your legs start shaking and cramping.

Use Binoculars

When you leave your original position and begin stalking, remember to use your binoculars often. Do this to check your objective buck's status, and locate other deer you didn't see.

I'll use my binoculars for the distance work of course, but also use them right down to ranges as close as twenty feet. It's amazing how much more detail you can pick out by doing this. Many-a time I've been stalking along and noticed something sticking out of the bushes ten yards away. At first glance with the naked eye I've discounted it as nothing of consequence. But one look with the binoculars confirmed the tine of an antler belonging to a deer I hadn't seen. While on the way to checkpoint two glass anything that looks suspicious or out of place.

JVN

Don't Peek After Checkpoint #2

After checkpoint number two, there's another very important rule to follow: Don't peek. One of the most disappointing things to have happen as a hard-working hunter on his own or as a guide sending a hunter on a stalk, is to have the stalk blown by "sneaking a peek" after the second checkpoint. So the rule is this: Never take a look at the deer you are stalking after you pass the second checkpoint! When you get to checkpoint number two, check to see if he's still there. Then, don't look again until you get into position at checkpoint number three.

When you do check the deer's position from checkpoint two and three, just look at the top of his antlers or a piece of the deer that doesn't include his eyes. If you can see his eyes, he can see you!

Sneaking a peek as you close in on the shooting position blows more stalks than any other factor, except for a swirling wind carrying your scent to the deer. Fortunately, you can control the "sneak a peek" variable by resisting the temptation to do it! A mule deer's peripheral vision is like radar – he will see any movement made in his entire amphitheater of vision. You know the deer's location as it relates to checkpoint number three, so concentrate on your foot placement and staying out of sight. Don't get busted three-quarters of the way through your stalk.

A buck experienced enough to have a rack like this is going to spot you if you "peek" after checkpoint number two; his peripheral vision is phenomenal. Resist the temptation!

Stalking In Stocking Feet

When you're bowhunting and you reach checkpoint two, quietly slip off your boots and slide a pair of heavy wool socks over your regular socks. The wool socks will quiet your steps by about 100% in the critical last stalking yards, and you'll really be able to "feel" your way across the terrain. In addition, pull the wool socks up over your pant legs to help keep them from swishing. But watch out for cactus! Lots of little ground cactus grows all over the West, and the surest way to find one is to take your footwear off. Jim showed me this "stalk in your socks" trick the very first time we hunted together, and my very first step was onto a cactus. We almost blew the stalk right there because I wanted to yell and he was having trouble holding back his laughs. But we ended up 12 feet from a 5x5 muley buck. That probably wouldn't have been possible had we been wearing lug-soled boots.

TJC

Getting Into Position At Checkpoint #3

While waiting for a shot at checkpoint three, pick a position that will allow you to move your legs slightly. Do this — without making too much noise — to restore your circulation as needed. If you're bowhunting, you could be waiting here a couple of hours. Even if you're rifle hunting, you might need to wait a fair amount of time for that deer to get into perfect position.

A position with both feet under you is a poor choice. If you're right handed and bowhunting, try sitting on your left hip and rear end, with both legs in front of you, bent at the knees and left thigh on the ground. That way, you should be reasonably comfortable for a long period of time, and can shoot from a sitting position or lean forward and up on the left knee to get ready.

Shooting a bow from a sitting position, on the ground, takes a little practice but works well. If another rest isn't available (rock or tree branch, etc.) and you're rifle hunting, a sitting position is about as steady as you can get.

Standing behind a tree, bush or rock at checkpoint three is also a good option, but is seldom available. Regardless of what position you have to take while waiting, make certain your bow is up in front of you, perpendicular to the ground. You'll want very little movement when it comes time to draw. Likewise, have your rifle at port arms. In either case, the actual amount of time you'll have for a shooting opportunity may be very short indeed. Don't get caught flat-footed.

Here's a special, important consideration for bowhunting. If at all possible, do not draw on a mule deer until his eyes are completely hidden from view. That is, wait for his head to be obscured by something — his body, a rock, a bush, a tree, a rise in the terrain, etc. That extreme mule deer vision will catch your movement every time. There are exceptions to the rule, but if you play it this way you will be far more successful. Chances are, the deer will hear you draw anyway and look directly into your eyeballs. But if his eyes were obscured when you drew, it's generally too late; you'll have time to anchor, set the pin and release a good arrow before he figures out what's going on.

Wait For The Right Shot

When rifle hunting or muzzleloading, make sure checkpoint number three provides you a full view of the deer or at least a clear, responsible shot at the vitals. If the angle of the shot isn't right, wait for the situation to develop. If you can do it without being seen, sneak to a different position to get a better shot. If you like the range and you have the patience, your best bet is to stay put, get a steady rest lined up and wait.

When bowhunting, checkpoint number three is the place you wait for an opportunity for a responsible shot. This position should not be closer than 20 yards or farther than 30 yards if you can help it. Make certain this position has a bush, rock, tree or something directly behind you to break up your image. There should also be something small in front to help cover you. Then wait. And wait some more. Wait for the shot to develop.

This tactic can't be overemphasized. Many bowhunters make a dreadful mistake at this point that costs them dearly. The mistake is forcing the situation by making the buck do something — like move, stand up, look away or anything else designed to force the situation.

You've taken the time to spot him, taken the time to make a perfect stalk, carefully crept within easy range and now you want to hurry things? Not smart! Wait for your opportunity, no matter how long it takes. That buck won't lie there all day. You want to wait for a calm deer out there in front of you.

Look at it this way. The average bowhunter will sit in a tree stand for hours and days on end, waiting for a whitetail. When the opportunity finally comes it's a matter of waiting for the deer to get into position for a responsible shot. In stalking, once you're in position at checkpoint three, there's no waiting for the deer to show up. He's already there. Now, all you have to do is wait for the deer to get into position for a responsible bow shot. And this wait is usually much shorter than the average tree stand vigil.

When you're this close to a buck, don't force the situation. Wait for the shot to develop, no matter how long it takes.

Here's what happens if you force the buck's hand.

If you do spook the buck by accident, bleat on a diaphragm call. This may present an opportunity for a shot. Be ready to shoot!

A buck gets tired of lying in one position and will eventually get up to change beds. Or the sun will creep over a ledge or overhang, causing him to move when his pleasant shady spot disappears or moves. Pesky bugs can also distract a buck and cause him to move. Occasionally the "boss buck" will come along and kick the one you're after out of his spot. Sadly, the boss bucks are not always the deer with the biggest and best antlers.

There is only one difference in waiting for a responsible shot after a stalk and waiting for a responsible shot from a tree stand – learning to handle a longer duration of adrenaline flow. Waiting at checkpoint three is a great and natural high. A little extra patience there generally pays off later!

Rifle and muzzleloader hunters can also benefit from waiting patiently and not forcing the situation. If you completed a successful stalk, that animal isn't going anywhere fast. A stationary, calm, surefire target is what it's all about. Make your hunt last a little longer, and end it with a cleaner and quicker kill.

A Classic Stalk

We've talked a lot about specific techniques and tactics for pulling off a successful stalk. We've discussed plenty of tips for making sure you don't blow your cover and spook the animal. Equally illustrative is an example of things done right, a narrative on everything coming together and working just so. One of my archery hunts provides such an example.

You'll find that no two stalking situations are exactly alike. Most often, you'll have to improvise. When you do, keep coming back to the basics outlined in this chapter – looking in the shade, scrolling and skirting, using the wind, using checkpoints, staying behind cover, refraining from peeking and waiting for the right shot – and you'll find that stalking can be both successful and fun.

I was hunting with Jim on a September day in central Wyoming. The stalking techniques outlined are second nature to him, and his ability was key to us getting that buck.

We had spotted deer in the early morning. Two mature bucks were feeding slowly through the sage toward one of the few creek bottoms in this rolling, high-plains prairie. The bucks were on the move and unapproachable. We returned later in the morning and began working our way slowly through the uneven terrain, scrolling and skirting and looking for the bedded bucks.

Crossing the narrow creek bottom — just some green grass and a line of cottonwood trees — two young white-tailed bucks bounded off, fortunately for us heading down the drainage, away from the draw's opposite slope where the muley bucks were likely to be.

One wash-out was visible in that entire sweep of new country, and we slowly worked our way up and around it, skirting below ridge crests and scrolling up bits of country from different angles. Finally Jim backed down and whispered, "Two bucks, bedded in the shade beneath those two big boulders." Since we were already at what would ordinarily be checkpoint two, we dared not take another look.

The opposite side of those two car-sized boulders was our checkpoint three, so we worked behind a rise to get into position to make the final approach. A steady westerly wind was in our faces. We closed to within 50 yards, keeping a careful eye on the rock pile to make sure the deer weren't getting up. Then we stopped to slip off our boots.

The bucks were bedded in the shade behind these boulders. We moved into the wind to get into position, then waited for the sun to get them up and moving.

The authors with just one of the rewards from a classic stalk on the Wyoming prairie.

With just socks on our feet, our final approach was almost silent, and an inadvertent swish of sage against pant legs was lost in the breeze. I side-hitched along in the sand to take up my final position, bow at ready in front of me. The bucks rested a mere 10 yards away, on the other side of the boulders.

We waited there over an hour with the midday sun beating down and the stronger wind gusts whipping sand into our faces. I thought of the bucks, not really believing I was this close to them, and planned out the ranges to different spots in our little amphitheater as the sun and wind burned my face. And I waited some more, bow at the ready.

The sun finally did its work, coming around and wiping out the shade patch. Jim's almost inaudible whisper from behind said, "Get ready" as I saw antler tines rising above the boulder. I shifted position to be facing the right way, before the deer came into view on my right, and drew.

All your thinking goes to hell in such a moment. All you can do is rely on instincts built on long hours of shooting practice. The buck, big and blocky and gray, emerged quartering away as I anchored. Though the movement was very slight, muley bucks see everything and I was out of place. As he turned to look at me the 20-yard pin found his last rib and the shot was on its way.

The buck bedded down 40 yards from where he was shot and his buddy, the bigger one of the two, stayed with him for awhile. Then they both went over the hill but my buck fell behind, slowly sinking into the sage as we glassed from the new vantage point we had scrambled to.

When we finally walked up to him the western sun was raking across the sage, now orange in the glow of late afternoon; that sun had done its job in helping me get this buck. I admired his 4x5 rack for a few moments. A few shreds of velvet remained. I marveled at how heavy and steel-gray and stocky the deer was. The never-ending wind, another aide to me this day, kept blowing and we turned the buck over and began our work in the quiet Wyoming sage.

TJC

Chapter 8

Other Hunting Methods and Tricks of the Trade

Introduction

Although spotting and stalking is the essence of mule deer hunting and we've covered those subjects in detail, there are other ways to successfully hunt mule deer. You should have some of these tricks in your arsenal of strategies and techniques. We'll discuss driving mule deer, still hunting and a special strategy we call "Stalk Over Here, Stand Over There." You'll notice that many of the spotting and stalking skills already discussed apply to these hunting methods as well.

As with all outdoor activities, mule deer hunting has its own tricks of the trade. These are tips and insights that will give you a real edge and help you improve your chances for bagging the buck of a lifetime. These are details, and details really count when you're dealing with a game animal as cagey and sneaky as a mature mule deer buck.

Here are a few of the bucks Jim has taken by paying attention to details, and by using the "tricks of the trade" in this chapter.

115

OTHER HUNTING METHODS

Driving Mule Deer

The phrase "driving mule deer" is, in some ways, a misnomer. When one uses the word "drive" it implies you're steering something to where you want it to go. You just can't do that with mule deer. They go where they want to go. "Pushing" mule deer might be a better way to say it. The best you can do is employ a sound strategy for working through breaks, draws, wash-outs, canyons, timber patches and brush, just like you and your hunting partners would do while chasing pheasants or whitetails. Before you start the drive, you'll of course have to set up strategically-located standers to wait in ambush for flushed deer.

The best time for driving coincides with the best time for stalking – the mid-day hours of 10

Planning a drive.

Part of the fun of driving mule deer is the chance to hunt effectively with friends and family. Success comes from a coordinated, group effort. This buck isn't huge but the hunt was fun.

or 11 a.m. to 3 p.m. or so. When the sun is straight up and is beating down on those thick gray mule deer coats, mule deer bucks will seek out places that are shady, cool and well-hidden. Hunting pressure might also send the bucks to these spots. In timbered habitat or other brushy terrain, these places are in the thickest stuff on the north slopes. In more open habitats look to the roughest, most cut-up country around. The only way to get the deer out and potentially into the sights of a stander is by "bumping into them."

Two people, one to push and one to stand, can accomplish a drive fairly effectively in wash-outs, breaks and medium-sized draws. Three or four hunters is probably a better number though, especially in areas of small timber and brush patches, where the deer have a lot more cover in which to sneak around. In most cases, you're better off with more standers than drivers. This helps to cover all the potential escape routes, especially if the driver is thorough as he or she covers the country.

Hunters should pick spots at the top or bottom of a canyon, draw, timber patch or other cover, to wait in hiding. These standers must make certain that an approaching deer won't catch wind of him or her, and should also look for natural saddles in the terrain that sneaky mule deer might use to slip into the next drainage.

The drivers then walk the area, one on each side of the draw, canyon or timber patch, keeping each other in sight. One of the keys to pushing muleys is to hunt small areas that are less than 700 yards or so in length. Any farther than that and the deer have too many opportunities to sneak out the sides before getting within range of the standers.

Of course, therein lies another stander's strategy. As we said, this is more of a "push" than it is a drive. If there are obvious saddles, draws or gullies that might make good escape routes even though they aren't directly ahead of the drivers' path, it may make sense to put a stander there.

Here's a package of does, followed up by a monster buck, squirting out of one drainage and into the next. A properly executed drive can move bucks like this into your sights if the drivers are willing to work the area thoroughly.

Use A Call

If you're bowhunting or photographing deer, each stander should carry a mule deer, predator or diaphragm call (the hands-free type). When the flushed deer gets within range, stop him with the call. A buck will often stand still for you for a few seconds, after hearing a grunt or light "sigh" on one of these calls. It's a sound he's just not expecting at that moment, and that curiosity factor can get the best of him. Have your bow drawn or your camera up and focused. The opportunity will be brief so you need to be ready. Rifle hunters can use this trick to try to stop a bouncing deer long enough for a shot; the deer only has to be close enough to hear the call.

Now, driving mule deer seems very simple and you're probably thinking everybody knows how to do this. But what many hunters don't realize is that, even though the drivers are moving downwind trying to get their scent to help move deer, and probably making a lot of noise, mule deer (especially big bucks) would rather "sit tight" than make a run for it. In addition, even though the wind is blowing directly from the drivers to the deer, the scent may not actually be reaching the deer. Surface interference can and does cause the wind to do strange things, like change direction with turns in the terrain, or even carry right over particular areas.

There are two bottom lines. Even if a deer smells you he may choose to stay put. And as a driver you're not out for a stroll, you're there to kick out a deer. Work the country with these facts in mind. Be aggressive. Do things that will get the deer's attention. Walk along the edges of draws, gullies and cuts, and look to the very end of each and every side gully and washout. Those areas containing shade are your best bet, but don't overlook any little hiding spot. Most hunters will say, "A deer won't get into a place like that, there's only one way out!" We guarantee they will go in there (see sidebar following). There's plenty of time for a nature hike once hunting season is over. On a deer drive hunt hard or you'll walk right past a buck and he'll be a good one. You can bet on it.

Sitting Tight

Here's a brief story about how tight mule deer can sit. This is just one of the many such instances I've witnessed. Who knows how many bucks I've walked past over the years?

An Oregon friend of mine, Wil Ward, and I were hunting not far from my Wyoming home. At daylight Wil and I bellied up to the crest of a ridge, peeked over ever so slightly and were thunderstruck to discover we weren't alone. About 300 yards away, on the face of the next ridge over, walked another hunter in our secret spot. Although disappointed, we decided to stay and watch the hunter's progress. (I said disappointed, not dimwitted. Knowing the caliber of bucks that inhabited this area and thanks to the position we commanded, operation "bird dog" had just commenced!)

We hadn't been there two minutes when we noticed a big five-by-five buck with about a 28-inch spread sneaking out ahead of our "bird dog." The buck, ears laid back, ducked into a washout, then trotted, body and head low to the ground, to the main drainage and hot-footed it away for all he was worth. He moved quickly and presented no shot so we let him go, but noted his direction. The advancing hunter didn't have a clue what had just happened!

I immediately began glassing the country just ahead of our flusher. Upon looking into wash-out that was nearly cave-like, my binoculars jerked to a stop on one of the tallest sets of mule deer antlers I'd ever seen. There, lying in the shade at the very back of that dirt cave, was a dandy buck! How he'd even got in there, I didn't know.

Just above the wash-out and along it's edge was the trail our "bird dog" was walking. As the hunter began to close the distance, I noticed the buck's head slowly swiveling, ears forward. He could hear the guy coming up the trail at least 100 yards away. Studying the wash-out, I could see the buck was lying far enough back under the overhang that unless he bolted, the hunter would never see him. Wil could have taken the deer from our position, but even though "bird dog" was out of harm's way, we decided no self-respecting hunter would shoot a buck from virtually under another man's feet. Oh, we would use him like a puppet, but that's as far as we would go!

We held our breath and watched the hunter walk along slowly, stopping every now and then to gaze at the surrounding landscape. Each time he moved the buck would listen carefully. When our pawn got right over the top of the buck, the deer swiveled his head around, looking straight up at the underside of the overhang and listening intently. I thought to myself, "This is going to be fun to watch no matter what happens!" As the man's shadow extended over the overhang and across the wash the buck's head whipped around, the animal's eyes locking on the shadow. The deer then laid his ears back, lowered his head and froze. I could hardly believe my eyes. Even as the hunter walked past, with

his scent flowing directly to the buck, the monarch never moved a muscle.

We backed up below the crest of the ridge, moved into a little better position, and waited for our duped comrade to get out of sight. Then Wil downed the buck in his bed.

What a great spectacle and learning experience for us both. It confirmed what we already knew about mule deer intelligence, but sometimes mistakenly doubt.

JVN

Wil Ward and his high-racked, cagey buck.

119

Still-Hunting

There is both art and science to the technique of still hunting. Sooner or later, in much of mule deer country, you'll end up still-hunting for the buck you want. Usually, this is a deer you have spotted and seen go into timber or other cover you can't see or shoot into. Remember that rough, cut-up country is cover too. On occasion, you might decide to move into a patch of cover on the hunch that a buck just has to be there.

In either event, you're going in to look for the deer and that's still-hunting. You're stalking an animal that is in the vicinity but you don't know its exact whereabouts. So, still-hunting is very similar to stalking except that you have to notch up the intensity level, if that's possible.

There are many elements to still-hunting, but they are fairly easy to break down into simple rules. What we'll cover first is the science of still-hunting. But there's also an art to the technique. The art of still-hunting is the way you pull all the rules together and work a piece of cover. Because it's an art, you'll want to develop your own hunting rhythm when you're in mule deer country.

The Science of Still-Hunting

Wind. Moving directly into the wind is best, but quartering into it or moving across will work, too. Besides carrying your scent away, another advantage of moving into the wind is that it carries away any small noises you make as you sneak along.

Thermals. If the wind is calm, use thermal air currents to your advantage. In the morning, thermal currents rise as the air warms; so try to stay above where you think the deer will be. In the evening, as the air cools, thermal currents sink; so hunt below where you think the deer might be. This means that in the morning, as the air is warming, you'd want to be up high in the terrain, working down into (or staying above) the rising thermals. In the late afternoon and evening, stay lower in the terrain and work up into (or stay below) the sinking thermals.

Bucking The Thermals Rule

As with any rule, the idea of hunting from the higher areas downwards in the morning and from the low-country upwards in the evenings, has exceptions. The major exception here is: Don't trust this rule too early in either the morning or evening. Here's why.

In the morning, the air must be warming for thermal currents to begin rising. This warming doesn't occur automatically at dawn, or even when the sun is first peeking over the horizon and rising in the sky. It takes awhile, usually an hour or two depending on the time of year, for the cold night air to start warming and rising.

The evening air usually cools faster than the morning air warms, but again, make sure the thermal flow is truly heading downhill before you trust your chances for a buck to this air flow.

An Idaho still-hunt illustrates the point. Jim Campbell and I got a later start than we wanted that morning from his Utah home, and crossed the border into Idaho as the very first rifle shots started booming in Utah's rifle opener. We had hoped to be in place on some juniper hills when the shooting started, but plan B — a still-hunt — would have to do now.

The sun was just coming up but the late-October night had been clear and cold — the thermals were nowhere near ready to begin rising. So Jim took one flank and I the other of a large, flat-topped, juniper-covered hill and we began working our way slowly to the top, still-hunting and looking for the bucks that either lived here or might be sneaking in from Utah.

About three-quarters of the way up, a single shot rang out from Jim's direction. After finishing my hunt to the top, I walked over and found him about where I thought I might find him, sitting next to a very large and very beautiful four-point buck. The buck had been bedded near the top of the hill, in anticipation of catching those soon-to-rise thermals, but our hunt to the top preceded the warming air. The buck had stood as Jim came silently into view, but Jim is quick with a rifle when he sees a buck he wants. The deer crumpled back into his bed at the shot. Plan B didn't work so badly after all!

We dressed and caped the buck right there, and then we pulled him downhill, right into the face of the now-rising thermals.

TJC

Jim Campbell and an Idaho "buck the thermals" buck.

Eyes. Use your eyes more than your feet while still hunting. Look more than you walk. When looking, use your binoculars a lot. Even at close range, binoculars will pick up detail your naked eye misses.

That's the science of using your eyes when you still hunt. The watchwords are "slow" and "careful." Slow means don't just glance at the cover or countryside, but pick it apart section-by-section. Careful means look for pieces and parts, the parts described in Chapter 3. Don't move to a new vantage point until you're absolutely sure there are no deer in your scope of vision. This means in front, to the side and to your rear. (You'd be surprised at how a muley buck will let you walk by, then exit out the back door. If you make a habit of glancing back, you'll catch one at it sooner or later.)

Profile. Keep a low profile as you hunt. This means you should never skyline yourself along a ridge – always hunt below the crest. Cross over ridges only in saddles, or on your knees or belly. And use the scrolling technique we discussed in Chapter 6 to survey new pieces of country. If you're still-hunting correctly, you'll be stationary more than you're moving. Whenever you stop to look and glass, make sure your profile is broken up by either a backdrop or cover in front.

The Art of Still-Hunting

How to use the wind, the thermals, your eyes and a low profile are fairly cut-and-dried rules for still-hunting. That's the science. But there's also an art to the technique. It's a feeling for how to bring all the above elements together and work through the cover at the right pace, quietly looking where deer are likely to be. The art also includes being constantly ready with your rifle, muzzleloader or bow.

Pace. How fast do you move through the cover? There are no rules. You'll have to get a feel for it. If you're blowing deer out of their beds, or just seeing white rumps going over the next ridge, you're going too fast. Letting your eyes do more work than your legs is always the best way to go. But when you do move, do it slowly and surely, staying behind cover of some kind and knowing where your next good stop-and-look point is.

Quiet. Wear the same types of clothing and boots you would wear for stalking (see Chapter 7). While you probably won't be taking your boots off, unless you spot a deer you want to sneak up on, make sure you can feel the ground through your footwear's soles. If you do make a noise, wait five minutes to let everything calm down.

Look in the right places. Concentrate your eye work on the high-percentage spots, like patches of shade and sweet spots you can identify. The more you're in mule deer country, the more you'll get a feel for areas that look like they would hold deer and those that don't.

Be ready to shoot. Have your rifle at port arms at all times. If you're hunting with a muzzleloader, be ready to prime your weapon. Hunting with an arrow nocked is a choice you personally have to make. It can be hazardous. At least be practiced in removing an arrow from your quiver and nocking it quickly and silently. These points can't be emphasized enough. You can literally be still-hunting along one second and, five seconds later, your deer will be on the ground. But that only happens if you're prepared to take the shot very quickly. It's amazing how quickly one can operate on auto-pilot. Help your instinct by having your rifle ready. Don't leave it slung over your shoulder. If archery is your game, have your bow in your bow hand and know which arrow you're going to take from the quiver when you finally see that buck.

The watchwords are MOVE SLOWLY if you want to still-hunt up to a buck like this.

Stalk Over Here, Stand Over There

The idea here is don't use both stalking and standing strategies in the same area. When you are hunting mule deer in a particular piece of country, divide it into two areas: a stalking side and a standing side. First determine from what direction the prevailing wind comes; then draw a line across your proposed hunting area perpendicular to the wind direction. The downwind half is the stalking area and the upwind half is the stand area.

No matter how good you are at stalking, you'll work on several mule deer before getting an opportunity for a responsible bow shot. Of course you'll blow a few stalks, but the variable that will most often stem your success is not being able to get a good, clean shot at the deer. With rifle in hand, the percentage goes up somewhat, but the task can still be tough. The only things that can improve your odds is

making sure to choose a high-percentage stalk (see Chapter 7). Every time you stalk you will definitely be moving a few deer from their beds, so why not take advantage of it?

Mule deer bucks will tolerate being "bumped" only a few times before they move to another area. Because you will almost certainly spook far more deer than you get an opportunity at, it is important to attempt to run the spooked deer from your stalking area over into your stand area. It is always difficult to predict where mule deer are going after they've been spooked, but you can bet they'll move out of an area where they are jumped every day.

Big bucks have a general tendency, once they decide to leave, to go up the draws and over a big ridge or divide, down into another major drainage. Chances are they'll do this

M.R. James with a velvet buck taken on the "stalking" side of the ridge.

movement into the wind as much as possible. If you have such a ridge or divide in the piece of country you've chosen, use it as your dividing line between stalking and standing areas, provided that the wind usually blows perpendicular to that ridge or divide.

If you're hunting in a group, have part of the group stalk and the other hunters stand. Trade off as the stalkers' tongues begin to drag the ground. This is a real nice technique for a pair of hunters to use. If you are by yourself, stalk for a few days, then stand for a few days in the new area.

The standers have a small disadvantage in that when the deer come from the stalking area to the stand area the wind is in the deer's favor. This is why it is important for the standers to use typical whitetail tactics to erase scent (cover scents, clothes washed in scent-free detergent, lots of camouflage clothing, if legal, and other precautions), and

place or take up stands in cross-wind situations as much as possible.

The logical time to be standing is while the stalkers are doing their thing and the deer are moving directly to the standing area. But the standing area can also be an excellent place to hunt later that same afternoon or evening, or even the next morning, once the deer have settled down in the stand area and are moving around in there to feed. The deer may even be up and about early in the day, trying to work their way back where they came from.

The "stalk over here, stand over there" formula is perfect for bowhunting situations, where hunting competition is low and you're generally the only hunter(s) in an area. The strategy is a good one for rifle hunting season, too. But be aware, mule deer sometimes travel a long way, and you may push some deer for other parties.

TRICKS OF THE TRADE

Avoid The "Educate 'Em Blunder"

A big mistake many hunters make when coming out West is showing up a few days before the season and intensively scouting their chosen area. It's okay to show up early to insure a good campsite and maybe get some fishing or relaxing in before the intensity of a rigorous hunt, but don't hike or drive through your hunting area the last few days before deer hunting season begins.

This goes for bowhunters, muzzleloaders and rifle hunters. Mule deer are smart. They get used to seeing particular vehicles and activities throughout the year. When there's a major increase in activity mule deer will get nervous and move out of the area immediately. This is especially true of the bigger, more experienced bucks!

Big bucks, although naturally nervous, become even more fidgety every autumn any-

way. Every year, around the same time, they begin to see more vehicles and more people. Before they know it they're being pursued heavily. A couple years of that treatment and they really do remember what's coming. All wild animals get accustomed to a certain amount of activity. Increase that activity or change its look and deer will notice. Here's just one example.

They Even Notice Hats

Here's an example of how mule deer get accustomed to certain patterns, and get nervous when something changes.

For years I worked irrigating a large series of hay meadows for a relative. The meadows always held several mule deer bucks, morning and evening. The bucks got very used to me walking around the fields doing my work. Eventually, they paid me hardly any attention at all – as long as I wore the same hat! If I showed up in a different hat, they were outta' there in nothing flat.

If muleys notice changes to their surroundings such as hats on a ranch hand, they're sure to get spooked when four-by-four trucks with grinding gears and loud-talking people invade their domain. So if you're traveling to mule deer country, select a good campsite a couple days ahead of time if you want, but don't drive or hike around in your hunting area. You'll only chase that big buck over into someone else's spot. If you can't stand not getting out there, glass from camp, tune your equipment and review this book. Save your stealth for opening day.

JVN

Scout Early

If you're going to scout and you're going to avoid educating the deer, do any scouting a few weeks ahead of the season. Remember that weather changes can move the deer around, so be flexible once the hunting season starts. If you'll be hunting an area where mule deer are resident and not very migratory, you could even scout a few months ahead of the season to get the general lay of the land and locate the deer-rich pockets and sweet spots.

Scouting Techniques

Scouting is a very important part of trophy mule deer hunting. When to scout is of the utmost importance. Scouting your area shortly before the season may alert those bigger, more experienced bucks and give them an opportunity to go into hiding. As a rule of thumb, scout from two months to two weeks ahead of the season. Any activity inside of 14 days before

the opener (unless you are very experienced), is risky. If you do bust a big buck out while scouting, 14 days will give him an opportunity to get back to his normal routine.

However, many hunters – especially those coming West from out of state – may not have an opportunity to scout ahead of the season. In this case it's our opinion you're better off to stay out of your chosen hunting area until opening day. Either glass, long-distance from camp; or camp in a place hidden from view of your chosen area and sneak up to a well-hidden lookout point and glass from one to two miles away.

The other option is to backpack into the area a couple days before the season, find a well-hidden lookout and stay put. Once you spot the buck of your choice "camp" on him until first light of opening day.

Keep in mind that mule deer bucks often change their habits as well as the country they frequent, with the changing seasons. So bucks you have scoped out during mid-summer may be occupying a different part of the country by the time the season opens. In arid areas (and much of the West is dry), many springs and reservoirs dry up in late summer and early fall; this causes the bucks to change locations and vary their daily routines.

The best definition of scouting is "secretly watching." While scouting, use all of the hunting techniques (especially skirting and scrolling) we have described in this book. It is very important that the deer you're scouting are not aware of your presence. This way you can observe them in an undisturbed state and take note of some of their favorite feeding and bedding areas. Mule deer bucks are notorious for frequenting the same areas year after year and many times a buck will use the same bedding site year after year whenever he's in a particular area. You can also note other habits that may prove beneficial to your eventual success, come opening day.

Once you've found a trophy buck (the one you're looking for), take note of his general demeanor as you watch. By noting the way he acts in the general course of his day, you can learn a lot about that particular animal and how to approach the area in which he lives. Again, use extreme caution in not letting the deer know of your presence and when you're done watching, sneak away undetected. The less you disturb the deer the more apt they are to maintain their normal range and habits. Keeping a journal during these outings, as mentioned before, is greatly beneficial in re-membering the habits and disposition of a particular buck.

A Character Flaw Consideration

Although big, mature mule deer bucks sel-dom make this mistake, all mule deer are sus-ceptible to a character flaw: They often stop for one or two last looks at what spooked them. Mule deer curiosity and boldness can get the best of them at times.

If you accidentally stumble into a buck or group of bucks – and you are as big a surprise to them as they are to you – drop to the ground immediately. Go to a kneeling or sitting posi-tion, as low as you can go while still keeping the deer in sight. If the deer haven't deter-mined for sure what you are, they will stop at some point, sometimes at close range, to check you out. Be ready to shoot, even if you are car-rying a bow.

If even one deer in a group knows what you are, all the deer will run simply because the others are running. By dropping down, your silhouette is cut at least in half, representing the height of many of the mule deer's other predators. Once out of what they think is four-legged predator striking distance, the less experienced deer that haven't pegged you will stop for a quick look. So hunker down and be ready.

This behavior is different from what many first-time mule deer hunters would expect, espe-cially if the hunter's primary experience is with

If you spook a buck, kneel down and get ready to shoot because he may stop for a look back. Your oppor-tunity window will be short, so be ready!

whitetails. Getting too excited when you jump some mule deer – and blazing away with your rifle or using that precious one shot in your muzzleloader – will only confirm the animals' fears and guarantee their flight out of the country. Remember this character flaw, get down and ready, and wait for a good opportunity.

If you jump a really big buck that is alone, or a group of bucks with an especially big buck among them, hitting the dirt might only give you the opportunity to eat dust! The oldest, really wary buck will generally have the entire group on edge and the other deer will follow him without stopping. But don't give up. You can still get nice, mature mule deer bucks by being a little patient. Don't waste time and ammo shooting at a spooked mule deer. A stotting mule deer is no easy target.

Stay In The Saddle

Always be on the lookout for a "pass" or "saddle." If you can't remember what one is supposed to look like, check back in Chapter 3. These natural funnels between canyons or drainages almost always have a well-used game trail which muleys will use for normal crossing and as an escape route. These saddles become natural areas to do a bit of stand hunting, especially if there is other hunter activity stirring things up nearby. If you ever decide to sit and watch for muleys, a saddle is a great place to do it. Also, when conducting drives of your own, post someone in a saddle.

If you hunt the same area for a few years, you will figure out which passes are favorites by referring to your journal and making note of the bucks that skylined themselves briefly while escaping through such openings. If you are unfamiliar with the area, just study the surrounding countryside. Note the lowest places along the ridges between drainages, and you can bet there's an escape route present. These dips are often subtle, but they're worth searching out.

Let The Deer Find More Deer For You

While you are watching any deer, including does, fawns, bucks you've decided not to pursue and bucks you're trying to figure out how to get to, take note of what those deer are watching. As they browse or survey the country from their beds, their attention will be drawn to various things as they watch for approaching danger. Quite often one of the deer you are watching will help you spot another deer you hadn't seen. That other deer might be bedded, feeding close by or clear across the country on a different slope. A mule deer's ability to pick up movement, even at great distances, is amazing. One deer will often tip you off to another's presence. Noticing the other deer is important not only because it may be a bigger buck, but also because the other animal certainly will be a factor to consider if you plan a stalk to the first deer you saw.

Keep It To A Whisper

Most people just don't realize that even normal voices travel an incredible distance outdoors. The thin, high, dry air of the West helps sounds carry even farther. It's amazing but you can sometimes easily hear guys talking a half-mile away. If the wind is just right you can hear them up to a mile away. If you can hear people talking that far away, think of what a mule deer can hear.

Normally most of this talking occurs after people get out of their vehicle and are reviewing their hunting plans for the day. Make your plan inside your vehicle on the way to your parking location, or at least do your talking inside the vehicle at the parking location, keeping your voices down. Work out a set of hand signals to be used once you're outside the vehicle. Then shut the doors ever so lightly and do not make any noise in your preparations.

It always happens that sooner or later, you'll be lying under the crest of a ridge waiting for daylight, when a vehicle pulls in a half-mile or better away from your location. The people get out, slam the doors and begin talking. Cuss under your breath if you wish, but begin watching intently for every mule deer around, buck and doe alike, to begin moving out.

Lose Your Hat

Most hunters don't realize how far above their head their hat sticks up. Think about this for a minute. From the center of the pupil of your eye to the top of your head is approximately six inches. Add the average hat to that (at least three to four inches, more for a cowboy hat) and you have no less than 10 inches of your head being exposed before you can see anything over the ridge you're scrolling from. So, in peeking over terrain or an obstacle with your hat on, you're giving mule deer a 10-inch head start on seeing your movement. Take your hat off when stalking or scrolling and minimize that giveaway. Also, peek around the edge of terrain or obstacles when possible. You'll get busted less often than you will peeking over the top.

Let Scent Do Something For You

When working a piece of country, you will often find yourself at the top end of a drainage, canyon or draw, having found nothing of interest. Then, when peeking over into the next piece of country, you realize to work it properly you would have to trek back down to the bottom before starting, to get the wind right. In many cases that just is not practical. So use this strategy on the next piece of country.

Scroll up the country to look it over, then slip over the edge and quickly take a seat below the skyline where you have a panoramic view. Sit for a least 30 minutes, letting the wind carry your scent down country through the draws and canyons immediately in front of you. If there are deer hidden below you,

they will wind you and begin to sneak out. Normally they won't bolt unless they get a big charge of your scent and are very close. Instead they will skulk out, stopping every now and then to try to figure out what stinks. This tactic can get you a shot at a buck if you are rifle hunting. If you are bowhunting, it can give you an opportunity to watch where the deer go and plan a stalk.

Vary The Pace

When traveling afoot from one piece of country to another, or while heading back to your vehicle, you will sometimes kick a deer out of his bed. If you note the normal pace of a fast-walking human and compare that sound to the stotting or pogo-stick bouncing of an escaping mule deer, you'll find them fairly similar. When another mule deer in an area hears that pace, they will jump from their beds, even when they can't see what's coming, and bounce away to higher ground to check out the commotion. So vary your pace and slow down a bit when you're just trying to get from here to there in a chunk of mule deer country. You will find yourself getting more opportunities at bedded deer along your route.

Gawk Not In Retrospect

It's a fact of hunting life that at some point you will spot a mule deer while driving your vehicle through your hunting area. This deer may be bedded or standing within a stone's throw of the road or trail. While driving around in your truck isn't hunting, sometimes the buck is a nice one and the opportunity is just too good to pass up. Maybe the hunting's been tough or the weather bad and a buck in the hand is better than one in the bush. So, if you want a chance at the deer, the biggest mistake you can make at this point is to stop and gawk.

It's a natural reaction to slam on the brakes as you try to scoop your chin out of your lap. But keep your composure steady and the vehicle moving. Act like you don't see the deer. Drive well out of sight. Hopefully there is a dip or rise you can get to in short order. Then quietly get out and sneak back for a better look. Most mule deer see moving vehicles all year long and learn to cautiously tolerate them. But once you've stopped and they see a Chinese fire drill inside the cab, they won't hang around long.

Lights Out

While we're on the subject of trucks, take the dome light bulbs out of the inside of your vehicle. Most mule deer in lower country have seen taillights and headlights before, and they won't pay much attention as those lights go by as long as there are not too many at once. But once you've stopped and opened the doors you produce a stationary light with shadows going back and forth as you ready your equipment. That kind of stuff becomes cause for concern to a smart mule deer buck. Those bulbs are generally easy to remove, so make certain you do it before getting into the field. Also try to park your vehicle under the edge of some terrain, hiding it from the country you plan to hunt. Then, if you have to use a flashlight to find some equipment, you are less apt to signal all the bucks in the area to high-tail it out of there.

Use A Human Decoy

Here's a stalking trick you might want to try if you're hunting with a partner. This is an excellent bowhunting strategy, and works well for photographing muleys too.

After finding a bedded buck you wish to stalk, have your partner take up a position out in front of the deer at 400 to 500 yards distance, staying out of sight until you have reached a predetermined position behind the deer. This position should be within 20 to 30 yards of the deer you're trying for. Never get closer than 20 yards, for this strategy; with that extra distance there's less chance the deer's eyes will pick you up while drawing the bow or focusing the camera. Also, the extra yardage gives you a small buffer, should the deer get up and come your way.

Your position should always have a bush, tree, rock or other cover as a backdrop to break up your image and, if possible, something in front to cover movement as you draw your bow or focus your camera.

Once you're in position, your partner should then move out into plain sight of the deer and walk back and forth, stop, sit down, get up, etc. The buck will usually become concerned after a short while and stand up for a better look before leaving. Make your move to shoot after the deer has stood up but while his attention is still focused on your partner.

Use An Elk Call

Yes, you read right, use an elk call when working through mule deer country, if elk frequent the area. Here's how.

As you're still-hunting or otherwise working your way through cover, or working through some cover en route to a deer you're stalking, you're sure to make noises of some type; everyone does. Calling occasionally on an elk call will put surrounding muleys at ease, because they'll attribute inadvertent sounds to elk passing through. Bugle a little bit if the elk rut is on, but don't overdo it. It is also effective to mew every now and then like a bunch of cow elk will do.

Use the call sparingly. Elk don't talk non-stop but they are very vocal creatures, and mule deer pay them little attention. It seems if elk are around, mule deer are often at ease, believing that things must be fairly safe.

Elk In Action

I first saw this trick in action on an elk hunt with Jim and his wife Perri. We were working through some high-country draws filled with pines, trying to get Perri in bow range of a big bull and his harem we had spotted at dawn. A fair number of muleys resided there, so we'd call regularly when working through the cover between meadows. At one point, we came upon a bedded mule deer buck, a big, old four-pointer, that must have heard us coming from a quarter-mile away. We walked behind him at a mere 15 yards, our heads on each other's backs like some big old six-legged elk, and he never looked twice. It was almost laughable.

We weren't hunting muleys that morning but the effectiveness of this trick was evident. That mule deer thought we were an elk and he would have presented a calm, unsuspecting target at spitting distance.

TJC

Judging Mule Deer Trophies

How to judge a potential Boone and Crockett (B&C) or Pope and Young (P&Y) candidate is a tough proposition for any of us. Of course, the more experience you have, the easier it becomes. Most of us with some experience can identify, with a glance, a huge, monster buck. You will also note that in this event, even the most experienced mule deer freaks will begin to stutter when they see a monster. But seriously, what is difficult to determine at a glance is a buck that is on the borderline of B&C or P&Y.

The B&C minimum for a "typical" mule deer buck is a net score of 190 and the minimum for a "non-typical" buck is a net score of

This Boone & Crockett buck net scores 190 5/8, with deductions. He just makes the book. Brow tines would raise his score by a minimum of 6 inches.

230. P&Y minimums are 145 for "typical" and 170 for "non-typical."

Mule deer are like almost any other trophy you'll hunt in that individuals possess certain antler qualities, but may lack other qualities necessary for optimum score. One of the most notable examples of this I've ever seen was while hunting caribou. Caribou bulls have a menagerie of varying qualities. They either have great tops, good length of beam, reasonable bez points, and then nothing for shovels or have great double shovels, awesome bez points, super length of beam and no tops. Finding a bull with all the necessary qualities to make the book – huge tops with lots of points, awesome length of beam, large bezes, and double shovels – is a major project. The same applies with mule deer bucks.

A "typical" mule deer buck, as classified in the record book, is a deer with four points or tines on the main frame and a brow tine or eye guard on each antler. (A big four-point with-out eye guards is also considered "typical.") A "non-typical" deer is one with extra points protruding anywhere from the main frame, as described (see photos). All non-typical points are deducted from the gross score if classified in the typical category and all non-typical points are added to the total score if classified in the non-typical category (as long as they exceed one inch in length).

Mule deer have a tendency to have either good (long) front points—the main beam and G-4 points—and bad or short back points (the G-2 and G-3). Or they have bad fronts and good backs. Sometimes they may have either of the above problems and in addition have too much width on the inside spread, with no mass.

Note: Keep in mind that mass is overrated considerably when judging mule deer bucks. A buck with extreme length in the main frame points will out score a buck with huge mass and shorter points. Mass is impressive, but don't let it fool you. In addition, spread is also

This very old buck sported a very interesting, multi-tined non-typical rack.

overrated because if the width of the inside spread is greater than the length of the main beam, the difference is a deduction.

There are many configurations that can lead to disappointment in total score, so it's a major project finding one with all the right characteristics. You're looking for good, deep-forked and long front points, great length of main beam, a spread that doesn't exceed the length of the main beam, deep-forked and long back points, brow tines and reasonable mass.

Here are some tips to help in determining the quality of a buck you're glassing. When judging a mule deer keep in mind that the

fronts points, that is the main beam and the G-4 points, along with inside spread, make up approximately two-thirds of the total score. So finding a buck with good fronts should be one of your first considerations.

Then look to make certain that the inside width of the rack does not exceed the length of the main beam. A good rule of thumb here is this: If the buck's rack is wider than it is tall, pass him up. Another rule of thumb here is that the average width of a buck's ears, ear tip to ear tip when in the forward position, is 20 to 22 inches. This is just a rule of thumb though, as this measurement can vary. Some

The beautiful buck in front has: deep-forked, long front points; great length of main beam; deep-forked, long back points; brow tines; and good mass. Shoot him!

bucks have wider foreheads than others and, as noted by taxidermists, ear length will vary as well.

Also, make certain the buck's main beam branches well beyond the tips of his ears (at least an inch or two) before turning back to the inside. The extra length here will help considerably in the main beam measurement (again, as long as the inside spread is not wider than the main beam is long).

Then concentrate on the back tines, the G-2 and G-3 points. Proportionately, how do they look in comparison to the fronts in both length, mass and the depth of forks? A buck with good proportion between fronts and backs will generally score better overall than one with notice-able differences ... unless those differences are noticeably larger, such as huge fronts and colossal backs or huge backs and even bigger fronts. At this point the "stutter factor" comes into play and you better go after him!

Now that's not to say that some bucks with huge backs and "crab forked" fronts (or vise versa) can't make the 190 minimum, because some have. But it doesn't happen too often. Although bucks that are well-proportioned are harder to judge, as there is little within their structure to compare to, they will generally always score better.

Next, look for the presence of the G-1 points, the brow tines or eye guards as some people call them. A buck without the G-1s can gener-

This is a good buck, but he has crab-forked fronts.

ally cost you a minimum of six inches or so in total score. Unless he can make it up in other aspects, pass a buck without G-1s.

In summary, look for big fronts (main beam and G-4) and check inside spread. Make certain inside spread does not exceed main beam length. These three measurements make up about two-thirds of overall score. Anything with a main beam of 25 to 27 inches, a G4 of 12 to 16 inches and a 24- to 25-inch inside spread, will go a long way toward that magic B&C number. (When looking for P&Y classification reduce numbers by approximately 25%.)

Next, check the back tines in relation the fronts. Look for a deep fork and good length in the G-2 as well as G-3 point. As a rule, a G-2 of 16 to 18 inches and a G-3 of 9 to 13 inches will help considerably in knocking on the record book door.

Although the G-1s seem insignificant, they can make quite a difference. Also, remember mass makes up a very small percentage of the overall score as compared to length of the main frame so, don't let it sway you too much. And last but not least, don't get too hung up on width if you truly want to put a mule deer buck in the book!

JVN

Chapter 9

Making the Shot

Introduction

This is a book about hunting, not shooting. But in the end, shooting is an important part of hunting. Your accuracy and efficiency with rifle, muzzleloader or bow can make or break your hunt's moment of truth. It's a lot of work to get within range of a good mule deer buck. You want to make the best of your opportunity. While we don't profess to be weapons or ballistics experts (there are plenty of good books and magazines that delve into wonderful detail on these important subjects), there are some basic premises to discuss when it comes to making your shot on a mule deer.

A Tough Customer

Mule deer, especially the mature bucks, are tough animals. Big, heavily muscled and tenacious, they, as one Colorado rancher succinctly put it, "...take a fair amount of killin'." To make that even more of an issue, mule deer are frequently found in spots where you want to drop them in their tracks. If they go more than a few additional steps they may fall into a gully or, worse yet, slide into a canyon where getting the deer out is going to be a much bigger problem.

With a bow and arrow in hand, you always need to make solid hits. Blood trailing is exceptionally difficult in the arid terrain the mule deer often calls home. Sand, dirt and rocks often dominate the ground, and blood soaks up or is extremely difficult to see. You need to make a good, hard, well-placed hit.

Of course, part of the key to dropping mule deer in the right place is not shooting at one if it's somewhere it will be difficult to haul out. Most mule deer are at least fairly near somewhere you wouldn't want them to go; that's just the nature of much of mule deer country. With rifle, muzzleloader or bow you have to place your shot right, and make it count.

Joyce Morlock with a good buck taken at 300 yards.

RIFLES

Caliber, Cartridges and Action

Caliber. A .243 is about as small as you want to go on mule deer, and that may be pushing the low end of the scale. You're just not packing much "whomp", to put it simply, with anything below .25 caliber. The .270 and .280 are good for muleys. The .30/06 Springfield, 7MM Magnum, and others in that class, are about the ideal mule deer calibers. They are fast enough to shoot flat, yet big enough to carry a substantial bullet. Many hunters come west with the big magnums; that's fine if you can shoot the rifle accurately enough to make a good hit that will kill the animal without destroying half the meat. To make a good shot you have to shoot without flinching. Mag-

nums sometimes make people flinch. A bad hit from a huge, fast, powerful caliber isn't going to make up for lost accuracy.

Bullets. Consider 100 grains the minimum bullet weight you'll want to use for mule deer, and that's even a little light. 130 grains is more like it . Plenty of hunters use a 130-grain bullet in a .270 Winchester. It's a good fast combo. You'll find most of the .30/06 and 7MM people shooting 140 to 180-grain bullets. 150- and 165-grain projectiles work well, too. They're big enough to hit hard and even buck the crosswinds a bit, yet lean enough to travel fast.

Action. As for action, a bolt action is the way to go, hands down. Bolt actions are accurate and reliable. You control ejection of the spent shell, and the lugs lock tightly to keep dirt out of most of the mechanism. This is not to say you can't bring a rifle with another type of action out West and hunt with it. If the caliber is right and you're accurate out to at least 150 yards, you could do okay. It's just that the bolt action is tough and dependable, problems are relatively easy to fix, and even if things go a little haywire you'll still probably have the equivalent of a single-shot and that's all you should need anyway.

Autoloaders and pumps just produce more problems in the field, especially out in the windy, dusty, boondocks of the West. Lever actions are a decent choice, but are hard to find in good mule deer calibers.

All this aside, if you could somehow classify all the mule deer ever shot with modern firearms, the lever action .30/30 Winchester is likely the gun/caliber combination that has killed the most deer, by far. That's because this was the rifle that won the West from the start. It put meat on many-a table in the process, and remained the weapon of choice well into the sport hunting days of our own century.

Scopes

In this day and age, a scope is almost considered standard fare on a rifle in mule deer country. A good scope will gather extra light in low-light situations at either end of the day, and is just heads-and-tails more accurate than any type of iron sights. See-through mounts may be good enough but they can cause sighting problems because they make your scope sit so high. Your best bet is to go with just a scope, then purchase a good scope cover if you're afraid of inclement weather. (The rubber, "inner-tube" type that protects the entire scope is ideal, but some hunters prefer the flip-up cap type.)

As with binocular and spotting optics, do not scrimp when purchasing a scope. If you're buying a weapon and need to keep the budget in line (like most of us), don't get all the fancy enhancements on your rifle and skimp on the scope. Instead, get a solid, base model rifle and go for extra quality in the optics.

What power? If you want a fixed power, 4X is probably about right. A 4X will bridge the gap between having an acceptable field of view for close-range shots and having enough magnification to take a longer poke. But good variable power scopes work wonders. One of them may be your best bet. A 2X-7X is excellent, and a 3X - 9X works but that 9X is on the high end of where you want to be.

Accessories

A sling is a must in mule deer country. Carrying a rifle long distances is just much easier with a sling. There will also be many times when you'll need your hands free to climb or descend steep spots or navigate rough terrain.

One drawback to a sling. You can easily become complacent and get caught flat-footed, rifle over your shoulder, while a surprise mule deer offers you a shot. By the time you've gyrated through all the movements needed to get ready to shoot, the deer is gone. So only use the sling to travel, not as a convenient resting spot for your rifle as you hunt.

Detachable swivels are great. On the last part of a stalk you'll want to detach the sling and put it in your pack or pocket, to keep it from dangling in your way as you crawl your way through the sage, rocks or brush. It also makes sense to detach the sling when going in to still-hunt some thick brush.

Shots

No two rifle shots at mule deer are alike. Many are downhill (remember to evaluate if you can get the deer out of there before you pull the trigger). Some are uphill. A few are on flat ground. The average distance is probably 100 to 150 yards. That's not spitting distance — you need to be able to shoot fairly accurately — but it's not outlandishly far, either. The message is this: Be prepared to shoot long, but you probably won't have to. If you practice and sight-in well, you should be able to hit your deer.

Much of mule deer country is steep. If you're taking the shot at a sharp angle, either up or down, you may have to aim a bit low on the animal. That's how the physics of the matter work; at a steep angle, there's not as much gravity pulling your bullet downwards and its impact will be a bit higher than expected. If the shot is very long and very steep, the effect may be that you just don't have to hold high on the animal.

Practice, practice, practice — with the cartridges you'll hunt with — and you'll come through those moments-of-truth successfully like Kathy Warner did.

Sighting-In

Sight your rifle in to hit a little high at 100 yards. Now "a little high" isn't a precise term and that's by design. You need to work with ballistics tables for the ammunition you're shooting to figure out where to sight in. The goal is to be a little high at 100 yards so that you're "dead-on" at 200 yards or so and only a couple inches low at 300 yards. That way, you can hold on the deer right where you want to hit him at all those distances.

Here's an example. A good-shooting, modern .30/06 shooting a factory powder load and 165-grain boat-tail bullets should be hitting about 2.8 inches high at 100 yards. This will put the bullet right on at about 230 yards, and a hair more than 3 inches low at 300 yards. That way, you can hold the crosshairs right on the deer all the way out to 300 yards, and still be in the kill zone. That small bit of variability – it's only about 6 inches worth, not even as big as your hand – won't matter a bit when it comes to killing that deer. A faster-shooting .270 might need only be 2.2 inches high at 100 yards, and it won't even be a full 3 inches low at 300.

Checking the Rifle

I guide a fair number of hunters every autumn, and I always have everyone check the zero on their rifle once in camp. But we don't get uptight about things. Usually, I'll line up a few dirt clumps a hundred yards away on a hillside, and have each hunter take a couple shots. If a hunter hits that clump, we call it quits and get ready in other ways. You need to check the zero on your scope when you get to mule deer country, but I figure if they're close enough to hit that clump they'll hit their deer on the hunt. I've seen too many people get rattled trying to make everything drop absolutely perfectly, at the last minute.

JVN

Shooting

Three words to mention here: Use a rest. If you're in open prairie country and the vegetation is low enough, a bipod attached to the front of your rifle works great. In timbered country, lean against a tree. If a rock is available, throw your pack or hat over it and use that. Place your pack on a sage bush and nestle in there. Sit on your behind and rest your elbows on your knees. Shoot from a prone position if you can. Kneel and rest your elbows on your hips if that works for you.

In short, use any and every method you can to steady your shot. Mule deer hunting is almost always a high altitude proposition; even much of the Western prairie is about a mile above sea level. Even if you're a native Westerner, you'll likely be breathing hard, and maybe a little tired as well. The wind will probably be blowing, too. It's all going to have an effect on how steady you can hold the rifle. Any help you can get in steadying your gun may make the difference between dropping the deer quickly, missing or worse yet making a bad hit.

The best way to assure a solid hit is to use a rest —any rest.

MUZZLELOADERS

Hunting with a muzzleloader is a fun and effective way to get mule deer, and many states offer special muzzle-loader-only hunts (see Chapter 13 for more information) where you can escape any semblance of a crowd and stalk muleys pretty much one-on-one. Your effective range – though not that of a modern rifle – still pokes out to a respectable 100 yards, 125 in some cases. There's some extra challenge in getting that close to a muley, but that's what makes the hunt extra-fun.

Muzzleloading for mule deer is exciting and effective.

Caliber, Bullets and Style

A .50-caliber is as light as you want to go on mule deer, with any style of muzzle-loading rifle. Sure, deer have been killed with a .45, but a .50 or something north of there just packs a bigger bullet and a bigger punch that is suitable for mule deer and those 50-yard-plus shots you'll likely get.

Part of the muzzleloader's effectiveness on mule deer stems from the large bullets you're sending out of that large-diameter barrel. Depending on what you're shooting, you may have anywhere from around 200 to 400 grains, or more, of lead flying through the air. 400 grains equals an ounce.

Traditional round balls have a proper place in some muzzle-loading hunters' arsenals. These plain '"pumpkin balls" fly fairly well at short to medium distances because of their relatively light weight (180 to 220 grains). But this is counteracted by the fact that their only spin comes from what's in the barrel; so these bullets' effective range erodes fairly quickly after 50 or so yards.

A better bullet choice is the modern conical bullet, weighing in at anywhere from 385 to 425 grains. These bullets pack a wallop because of their sheer size, and because it takes a lot of powder to send them on their way. They fly fairly well despite that size, because of their streamlined shape and the extra spin they get from being partially rifled themselves (in addition to taking advantage of the barrel's rifling). Conical bullets also load quicker than balls, which is valuable if you're getting an opportunity for a follow-up shot.

Midway between balls and conical bullets are the sabot bullets frequently shot from modern in-line firearms. The bullet is carried in a plastic sleeve which engages the rifling and stabilizes the bullet. This sleeve falls off as the bullets leaves the muzzle. Usually weighing in the 240 to 275 grain range, these bullets fly very well and are probably the per-fect match if you're going to tote a modern in-line muzzleloader.

The style of muzzleloader you carry is totally a matter of personal preference. Check game laws to make sure that modern in-line weapons are allowed in muzzle-loader-only hunts; in some cases they are okay, but regulations change with the times.

The modern in-line muzzleloaders are fine, but there seems to be something extra special about stalking muleys with a replica weapon – a percussion caplock in a traditional style, or even a true flintlock. Because ignition is never a given, muzzleloader hunting is always exciting. Perhaps it's also the idea of being out there with a little extra challenge added, chasing mule deer the way the mountain men did. The more traditional caplocks and flintlocks just seem to add some romance to the hunt. It's fun to imagine yourself as Jim Bridger, Jeremiah Johnson or Meriwether Lewis (of Lewis & Clark fame) alone in the pristine Rockies or wilderness prairie, and chase deer descended from the very same stock those men hunted.

Accessories

Your standard possibles kit is essential; be prepared to clean all parts of the weapon and make repairs far from any road or gunsmith.

Shots

As usual, it's hard to predict exactly what kind of shot you'll get, but 100 yards is a good maximum to prepare for. In reality, 50 to 75 yards is probably about the average shot you'll take at a mule deer with a muzzleloader, and this is a good distance to close to when stalking a deer. You'll get a nice, certain shot at a range that you should be able to connect on.

Sighting-In

Sight in for 100 yards and you should be able to hold right on that deer from point-blank range out to that point. While 100 yards is a good maximum shot to limit yourself to, experienced shooters may go for 125 yards; if you're confident and consistent, go for it. Otherwise, if you can work up a load that will consistently place your bullet in a deer's boiler room at 100 yards, you'll be in great shape.

Shooting

As with modern rifles, a rest is very important with a muzzleloader. It might even be more important because most muzzleloaders weigh more than modern rifles. And, you've only got one chance to make a good shot.

BOWS AND ARROWS

Mule deer hunting with archery gear is exciting. Usually a spot-and-stalk proposition, there is always a lot of action in the hunt, and you'll make many stalks before coming up with a successful one. But even then, you have to make good on the shot. With a bow, this a critical aspect of the hunt.

Bow Styles and Draw Weight

As far as bow styles go, personal preference prevails when choosing. The key factor is this: Do you shoot consistently enough, up to your self-imposed distance limitations, to be confident at making the shot? That confidence level

Jim Van Norman and a nice mule deer buck he took with bow and arrow.

is of the utmost importance when drawing back on a big mule deer buck after a lengthy stalk or a long wait on a stand.

Modern compound bows are definitely the weapon of choice for most mule deer hunters, because they're so fast, shoot so flat and hit so hard. If you're a whitetail bowhunter, your whitetail gear should be just fine for mule deer. The key here is that you be ultra-familiar with your equipment. Of course recurves have their place and you'll find many in mule deer country every year. Longbows are probably as common as recurves in mule deer country, and there are always a few traditionalists out with stick-and-string. These are usually very dedicated hunters who work hard and take their hunting and their archery very seriously. They get deer.

Consider 50 pounds the minimum draw weight you should use with any of the styles of bows. On a compound, this initial draw weight will still give you good speed and pen-

Good stalking techniques, well-tuned arrows and sharp broadheads produce bucks like this.

etration, especially if your arrows are tuned right. With recurves and longbows, this is also a respectable pull weight. To be able to get good penetration on tough muleys, and shoot out to 20 yards or so, you need this kind of energy behind your arrow.

Arrows and Broadheads

Here's a subject fraught with opinion and a complicated myriad of choices!

A discussion here could go on for pages, but the best advice is – buy the best arrows you can afford, then practice and hunt with the exact same ones. Sighting-in with broadheads, after you've got your field points shooting right, is a must. Take your best arrows from your practice lot, and use them on your hunt; a few frayed fletchings won't matter. If you insist on using brand new arrows on your hunt, test them first.

Most of today's aluminum and graphite arrows are excellent. Be sure to get help at the pro shop or from charts, to help select the best arrow weight and fletch configuration for you. Recurve and longbow carriers will frequently be seen with cedar shafts to match the more traditional nature of their bows.

As for broadheads, there's no secret here. If they fly well for you and you have them honed to a razor edge, use them. Whether they're fixed-blade or one of the modern insert varieties, they will do the job if they fly straight and cut well.

Sighting-In

If you're using pins of any type and can keep them straight, sighting in at 10-yard intervals is best. Ten, 20 and 30 yards are good choices. Fewer pins are okay, if you know how to make the slight adjustments needed when your animal is not at a convenient distance. Take some shots at point blank range too, and figure out which pin to use when a deer is incredibly close.

Averages and Extremes

Most bow-shot mule deer are taken at about 20 yards. This is probably a function of two things. One: It's as close as even a good hunter should get to a bedded mule deer without being detected. Two: It also coincides with the distance at which most hunters are still pretty darn consistent and deadly with an arrow. Beyond that, and things get a little more "iffy" for most of us. There are just more variables as distance increases. Nevertheless, I've been in on hunts with mule deer arrowed as close as three yards and as far as 42. I recommend setting a responsible limitation for yourself, and this usually tops out at 25 or 30 yards for almost all of us, especially when the adrenaline is flowing and the target is a live deer.

JVN

Shooting

About 30 yards, in our opinion, is about a maximum shot for any mule deer bowhunter. The only real secret here, other than good fundamentals brought about by hours of practice, has been mentioned already but bears repeating. Don't draw on any mule deer that is looking in your direction. The deer will use that incredible peripheral vision to catch your movement, and go on the alert.

Estimating the Range

Here's a tough one – estimating range in the wide-open spaces of the West. These judgment errors are often made on the long side. Hunters believe the deer is farther out than it really is and often shoot over its back. I was guilty of this a couple times, before finally connecting on a 20-yard shot. I knew the shot was 20 yards because I had plenty of time to think about it. But incorrect range estimation can go the other way, too. A good buck is so big in the body that you may think he's closer than he really is.

The solution? Practice, practice and practice some more. Estimate range as you jog, when you're walking somewhere, as you mow the lawn, when you're out playing with the kids, while small game hunting, on the golf course (I don't golf but it would probably work). Practice any time you're out in the open.

TJC

Here's Jim Sloat's reward for correctly estimating the range on this Wyoming buck.

SHOT PLACEMENT

Shot placement is also important on mule deer. Like we've said before, they're tough and they're strong and you often need to drop them at or near the spot at which they're standing or bedded. The following advice and photographs should help you make the most of these typical opportunities.

Broadside

Broadside. With a rifle or muzzleloader, shoot for the shoulder (1). The goal is to break that shoulder and push the bullet through to the deer's chest cavity as well. Breaking a shoulder is the best way to anchor the deer in its tracks, or close to them. With bow and arrow, you'll want to hit a little farther back (2), because most arrows are not likely to smash through a shoulder to get to the boiler room.

Quartering Toward. With a rifle or muzzleloader, shoot for the near shoulder (shoulder facing you) in an attempt to break it and have the bullet pass through to the chest cavity as well (1). With bow and arrow, this is a risky shot at best, because the deer will likely see you draw and you have little to no margin for error in aiming for the base of the chest or behind the shoulder; best bet—wait for a better opportunity.

Quartering Away

Quarter Away. With a rifle, muzzleloader or bow, shoot for the far shoulder (1). Imagine your bullet or arrow angling a path through the deer's chest cavity and then breaking (or at least hitting) the far shoulder. With a firearm, you may well break that far shoulder and save yourself a tracking job. This is the bowhunter's dream shot; the quartering-away deer is less likely to spot your draw, many vitals are exposed, and there's a small margin for error.

Straight On

Straight On. With rifle or muzzleloader, shoot for the base of the neck (1), trying to drive your bullet right into the chest cavity. Bowhunters would best pass on this shot.

Straight Away (A responsible hunter will not attempt this shot.)

Straight Away. Not a good shot for any type of weapon. But have your rifle up or your bow drawn, and be ready to pull the trigger or release your arrow when the animal turns, either quartering or broadside.

Chapter 10

The Work Begins: Field Care

OVERVIEW

When you walk up to a big gray mule deer and realize you really have done it – you really have bagged one, you'll also realize that now the work begins. While the hunt up to this point may have been difficult, it should also have been intense, exciting, thrilling and just plain fun. You've made an investment in time, money and sweat to bag this deer, now you have to work to preserve your trophy. This is a critical part of the hunt.

The care and handling of a mule deer is in most cases similar to the handling of its eastern cousin, the whitetail. However, there are additional demands unique to hunting mule deer in the harsh and expansive environments of the West. In short, the country is big and you may be very far from camp, a vehicle, town or locker plant. You'll need to rely on yourself to take care of the meat and trophy, at least initially.

In almost all cases when hunting on your own, you should be self-sufficient in your ability to care for your trophy in a manner more thorough than is required of the typical whitetail hunt. So this chapter serves as a primer for the hunter visiting the West to hunt its native deer. But the ideas here also serve as a refresher course for the native or resident Westerner who already knows the challenges involved with assuring prime meat and a beautiful trophy from what is often a jumbo-sized muley that's been dropped in rugged country, far from any two-track road. These deer can be killed in the hot sun of the desert, the treeless expanse of the prairie or high in the mountains; hunters need to be ready for the inevitable struggle of getting the venison to the butcher and the trophy to the taxidermist.

The work of the hunt isn't finished quite yet for guide John Spaulding and happy hunter Scott Trelstad ... especially considering the warm temperatures here.

One Size Doesn't Fit All

Mule deer are harvested in many different situations – that's what makes every hunting story unique and interesting. Each situation requires different field handling of the animal. The distance you must haul your deer to get it out of the field defines the situation, but the extremes of Western weather and terrain make these post-kill skills even more important.

As a mule deer hunter, you'll need to consider field care options and plan for them before the hunt. Then you'll be prepared to care for that prime venison, and work toward a perfect cape for your trophy, regardless of the circumstances and what the weather is throwing at you this minute.

A Crash Course

We'll describe some situations under which mule deer are typically bagged, present options for field care once an animal is on the ground, and detail specific methods and equipment you'll need to properly care for a deer in the field.

We don't consider the use of horses here, although horseback hunts are a Western tradition for some hunters. Horses are not available to most hunters unless they hire an outfitter, who then generally handles all the field care anyway. In any event, using a horse does not change the need for proper and prompt field care.

A horse simply saves some time, energy and your back while transporting a deer from the field.

SITUATIONS IN WHICH MULE DEER ARE HARVESTED

The Long Haul

Imagine this.

You've been glassing all morning and finally locate a nice four-by-four buck at high noon. You plan your stalk carefully, pick up your bow and start circling to get the wind in your favor and begin your sneak. An hour later you're there, arrow nocked, and a half hour after that the afternoon sun swings around enough to hit the buck. He stands up to stretch and find a new patch of shade to hide from that irritating sun.

This buck, though not huge, was not easy to get off the mountain because he was shot at timberline. At least the trip out was downhill!

Whack! He doesn't know what hit him and soon you're kneeling next to the grayest, most beautiful, blocky, big-antlered buck you've ever seen. But then you realize you're also looking at 225 pounds of meat, innards, skin, bones, head and antlers, and you're 3 1/2 miles from camp, and most of those miles are steep and rocky.

In such a situation you'll need to provide all necessary care for the trophy including field dressing, caping, skinning and breaking of the carcass.

There are still many opportunities in the West to hunt in remote areas and get into big bucks and challenging situations like this. Many restrictions close backcountry roads and completely exclude motorized vehicles to a relatively large (and thankfully expanding) amount of Western public land. These restrictions protect the fragile environments of the arid West, and provide a quality hunting experience away from crowds and noise.

These places are well worth hunting because the bucks grow big and old there. The spot where one of those bucks falls is one which you will long remember. You need to know how to care for the animal properly.

Easy Does It

At the opposite end of the spectrum, a good number of mule deer are harvested where a hunter can get a motorized vehicle, either a truck or four-wheeler, close to the animal. This is often the case on private ranches when the landowner agrees to allow limited vehicle access. Areas of public land where this is possible may harbor good populations of deer but rarely hold the biggest, mature bucks because access is simply too easy and hunter pressure is too high.

A typical situation here might be a rifle hunt where you shoot your deer in a sage meadow on a badlands ranch, and drive right up to him after walking back for your vehicle.

Or maybe you park your vehicle at a trailhead in the morning, and head up a mountain. You're working your way along a canyon side, just below the ridge, but not seeing any deer. At noon you cross over some meadows into another drainage, and hit pay dirt.

This canyon is less accessible, and the deer are holed up here. At 3:00 p.m. a nice forkhorn feeds out into the shadowed chaparral from a stand of spruces. One shot drops him before the echoes of your shot escape the steep sides of the canyon. After field dressing him, the downhill pull to the mouth of the canyon is fairly easy. Then you walk the two miles back to your truck, and drive the gravel roads at the mountain's base back around the mouth of the canyon, and load up your deer.

Somewhere In Between

The third situation straddles the distance between the previous two extremes. You don't need to pack the deer many miles to get it to camp or a vehicle, but you can't drive very close to it either; and a long uphill or cross-country drag is just not feasible.

Although distances may vary, the common ground is that you will need to transport the animal from the field over some rough terrain, often during weather extremes of heat, snow, rain or some other offering. This situation often occurs when you drive into an area on secondary roads, possibly set up a camp, and hunt out on foot from there. Proper care of the animal between when it hits the ground and when you can get it back to camp, and then to professional butchering and taxidermy services, is critical.

OPTIONS FOR FIELD CARE

No Guts, No Glory

Once the animal is down, approach it cautiously and confirm that it is dead by tapping an eye with an arrow, stick or your gun barrel. Bleeding the animal by cutting its throat is not necessary and, in truth, is not effective once the animal's heart has stopped pumping. Certainly do not bleed the animal if it is to be caped for mounting by a taxidermist.

Immediately field dress the animal, although in some situations (to be discussed), delay the field dressing until after caping. Proper and quick field dressing is important to ensure you get top-quality meat. Cool that deer fast!

Field dressing methods are familiar to most deer hunters and we'll review them later in this chapter. However, hunters from the Midwest, East or South may never have had to tie a deer to a rock or tree before field dressing. This is a common practice with mule deer hunters, keeping the deer from sliding deep into the "canyon from hell", the crossing of which may have occupied your time for the last two hours. Imagine getting a deer out of there.

Most field dressing methods outline splitting the chest and pelvic bone to aid in cooling. Note that if the animal is to be dragged from the field, delay this step until reaching camp or a vehicle. Waiting to open the carcass like this will minimize contamination with dirt and debris as you drag it.

Specific field dressing instructions follow toward the latter part of this chapter.

Be ready for a follow-up shot at all times.

One to Remember

If you want a shoulder mount of your trophy, cape the deer where it lies, even before field dressing. Do not drag the deer until it is at least partially caped. Any dragging, even to get the deer into a better position for field dressing, leads to breaking and chaffing of the hair, especially on the shoulders. This cannot be repaired and is the most common defect of capes delivered to taxidermists.

If the weather is cool, and if the cape can be taken to a taxidermist within 24 hours, partially cape to the base of the skull and there tie the roll of hide in place with twine. You can move a partially caped buck with only minimal concern for the cape.

If the weather is warm, or a taxidermist is more than 24 hours away, fully cape the animal. Again, it is most important to at least partially cape the animal immediately after death to avoid hair slippage. The hide, especially in the neck area, just does not cool fast enough to prevent slippage unless it is removed from the carcass. Even in freezing weather, the insulation provided by the hair keeps in enough heat for bacteria to grow and cause the hair to slip. Areas of the animal that are in contact with the ground or snow are also prone to hair slippage, because of the additional insulation provided.

Specific caping instructions follow toward the latter part of this chapter.

The Naked Animal

Your next important consideration is whether to skin the animal in the field before transporting it to the camp and then home or to the meat locker. If you've caped the animal, half the decision has already been made.

Leave the hide on if temperatures permit. This will protect the meat from dirt, debris and moisture loss as you get it out of the field.

The ideal situation is for the carcass to cool to less than 40°F less than 24 hours after death. This ensures the quality and wholesomeness of the meat, and that the muscles are well started on the pathway by which they are converted to meat. Thus, the time it takes to get to camp and then to the locker plant and the air temperatures expected during the next 24 hours, are the primary considerations when deciding to skin in the field or not. In most of the Western mountains, foothills, breaks and prairies during mule deer gun seasons, overnight temperatures are often less than 40°F and a skin-on carcass will cool sufficiently overnight. If nighttime temperatures are higher than 40, as is the case during many of the early season bowhunts, you should skin the deer, wrap the carcass in a game bag and then tie the bag shut to keep out the blow flies.

Whether you skin or not, take special care to keep the carcass in the shade during the day. It does not take long for the Western sun to cook meat and spoil an entire quarter or side of a deer.

Bits and Pieces

Your final decision is whether to take the carcass from the field intact, in quarters or as boned meat.

Transport the intact carcass, skinned or not, if the situation allows. This will maximize your options for aging and additional processing, and care of the animal is certainly more convenient back at camp or at the meat locker.

Dragging a whole carcass from the field is, unhappily, an exhausting activity and it is of-

tenphysically impossible for a single hunter if the animal must be moved uphill. This is especially true when you consider that a mule deer is even larger than a whitetail who has been around for as many seasons. Nonetheless, many deer are pulled out of the mountains or over the prairies and through the breaks each year by hunters who have followed the sage advice of "hunt uphill, drag downhill."

If the pull is short, consider yourself lucky or smart or a little bit of both. Grab an antler or tie a rope around the deer's neck and start pulling. A deer dragging harness, that goes around your shoulders and allows you to really lean into the chore, works well too. Just remember that with any of these rope options, keep the rope between you and the deer short enough so that the deer's front shoulders rise off the ground. Less of the deer on the ground means less friction and an easier drag. Every bit of energy you can save makes a difference in rough terrain.

Another trick that many Western hunters use is to whack off the deer's lower legs at the knee joints. These parts have no meat anyway, and are usually considered waste; getting rid of them will reduce friction and catching on brush, tree trunks and rocks.

Tying the carcass on a sled makes dragging easier. These sleds, made of tough plastic with a rope lacing, are available at many sporting goods stores and from most of the large catalogers. At less than two pounds, it makes a valuable addition to your day pack. In fact, using a sled makes dragging downhill so easy your main concern will be getting run over! So it's a good idea, when heading downhill, to have a second hunter man a rope tied to the sled's rear. The sled also protects the hide from abrasion, and a skinned carcass from getting dirty.

If you want, use a mechanical carrier to take the carcass from the field. The best of these are two-wheeled devices that follow the principle of a travois and are designed for use by one or two hunters. These devices are able to negotiate some surprisingly rough terrain on trails, but are of limited usefulness off-trail and in the rugged back country. Another drawback is that you can't just lug one around as you hunt; you have to return to camp or your vehicle to retrieve it.

You'll have to cut the carcass into quarters (instructions follow) if terrain or distance dictates that the whole animal is just too much to haul from the field at one time. Boning (discussed next) is another option here.

Quarters can be aged and allow for some flexibility in processing, but they do require you to carry a good deal of inedible material with the meat. On the other hand, a quarter is a lot easier to get out of a ravine or up a hillside than is an entire deer! The quarters from a good-sized mule deer of 200 pounds live weight are about 35 pounds each.

Strap the quarters on a pack board for carrying to camp or vehicle. At least three trips are necessary to transport the quarters, cape and antlers of a trophy mule deer: two quarters, two quarters, then the head and cape. You have to be in pretty good shape, and have a good pack board, to pull this one off. You're probably better off planning for four or five trips.

Don't hog all the fun. Instead recruit any help you can muster. Because any helper will want to see exactly where your deer was taken and how you did it, you can usually get help for at least one trip. Every hunter is interested in seeing the where and how of a successful mule deer hunt. If you are lucky enough to have helpers, strap two quarters on your helper's pack and don't take any excuses about bum knees, blisters or a recurring case of malaria!

No Bones About It

Boning the carcass (instructions follow) is the most efficient way to prepare the meat for transport to camp or a vehicle.

First skin the deer. Keep the carcass on the clean, separated hide or else place the deer on a plastic sheet to keep the meat free of dirt and debris as you work. Do not bone the meat until it has thoroughly cooled and has completed rigor (stiffening), usually about 12 to 18 hours after death. Use this time to skin the deer if weather dictates, and also transport hide and antlers to camp or vehicle. Be sure to recruit a companion for your return trip!

When you return to bone the carcass – probably the next day – place the boned meat inside bags that are lined with a double layer of plastic bags. Large food storage bags are best. If you do use garbage bags, make sure they haven't been treated with any sanitizing chemicals. Make sure your companion's pack is loaded with the heavier "half" of the meat.

Close the bags during transport to prevent leakage of any meat juices, but open the bags immediately upon reaching camp or vehicle to prevent the build up of moisture on the meat. Any condensation on the meat's surfaces provides an ideal breeding ground for the bacteria that spoil meat. Keep the boned meat cold and it is will remain wholesome for several days. The boned meat from a deer of 200 pounds live weight averages less than 50 pounds, and with the help of a companion, is easily transported in a single trip.

Keep the Coyotes and Bears Away

Hunting in areas where grizzlies or many coyotes live may make waiting 12 to 18 hours difficult, if not impossible. One trick to keep coyotes away for a night is to leave an item of your clothing (preferably one that's all sweated up) on the carcass. You might also try urinating around the perimeter of the area. If grizzlies are present, don't count on these techniques. Your best bet is to get the meat off the mountain quickly and for heaven's sake, if push comes to shove, don't fight any bear for your mule deer.

The Meat of the Matter

Once it is taken from the field, maintain the carcass, quarters or boned meat at 28 to 35°F until they can be cut, wrapped and frozen.

Hang an intact carcass or quarters to aid in cooling and drainage. Meat can be aged for seven to 10 days, if you so wish, at these temperatures. If outside temperatures are above 35°F, get the carcass or quarters to a meat locker as soon as possible.

Aging of venison is a controversial issue. Aging allows meat's natural enzymes to do their work and tenderize the meat. Meat will also develop flavor during this time. But the longer the meat is aged, the greater the risk of spoilage and the greater the losses due to evaporation. Also, not everyone prefers the flavor of aged meat. If you or your family are only marginally fond of venison because of its flavor, aging the meat for a shorter period may improve the taste for everyone. On balance, no more than four or five days of aging are recommended.

Do not age boned meat. Instead cut, wrap and freeze the boned meat as soon as possible. The once-sterile areas of the meat were contaminated with small amounts of bacteria during the boning process (this is a natural occurrence and does not harm the meat in any way), and boned meat spoils in a few days even at temperatures found in a meat locker. If temperatures are warm at camp, delay spoilage by putting the boned meat on ice in a cooler.

METHODS FOR FIELD CARE

Field Dressing

Field dress the deer as soon as possible after the animal is killed. This starts the carcass cooling and helps to ensure good meat. One school of thought says you should not remove the scent glands from the rear legs before field dressing because the secretions there may contaminate your hands and knife, which could, in turn, taint the carcass. You'll often hear another school of thought that says remove those scent glands immediately as their secretions will taint the meat if they are not removed. The choice is yours and the safest bottom line is this. If you do remove the glands, make absolutely sure your hands and knife blade are clean before proceeding.

Wearing plastic gloves is a good idea, especially if you have any open cuts. The gloves prevent even the remote possibility of contracting disease. Note that some mule deer, especially when harvested in milder weather, will have ticks. These ticks do not in any way affect the quality of the superb venison inside, but be sure to check yourself thoroughly for ticks after field dressing the deer.

Here's a brief field-dressing primer.

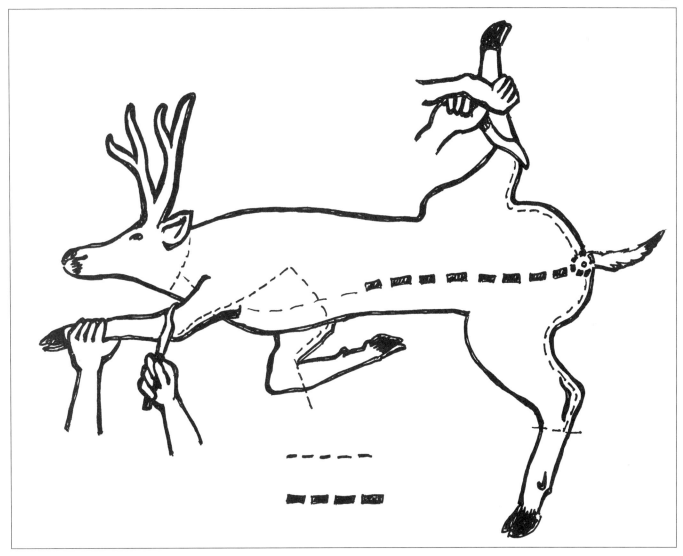

Basic cuts for field dressing (bold lines) and skinning (fine lines). Note also the cuts to make to take off the lower legs.

Roll the deer on its back and elevate its front end. Spread the rear legs and place rocks or sticks to hold the deer in position.

Cut entirely around the anus with a knife. Pull out the rectum and tie it shut using kitchen string. Place the tied end back inside the pelvis.

Cut away and remove the testicles of a buck and the mammary gland of a doe. In some cases, these must be left on the largest part of the carcass as proof of sex. Check the regulations for the area where the deer was harvested. Peel back the penis of a buck, splitting the hams slightly, and peel it back far enough so it can be inserted into the hole you made when you cut around the anus. This will ensure that the penis and bladder come out when you pull the rectum through.

Open the mid-line from pelvis to breast bone, taking care not to cut into the paunch and intestines. To avoid cutting into the paunch, make a 4-inch incision near the pelvis, pinching and lifting skin away from the body cavity as necessary. Complete the incision to

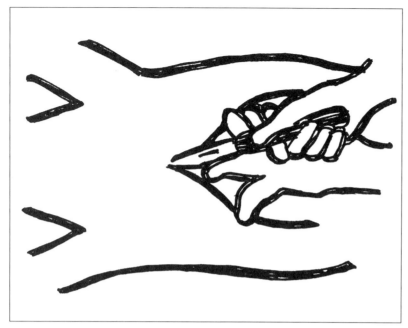

Lift the skin away as you open the body cavity. This is one of the keys to neat field dressing and good meat later.

the breastbone by cutting from inside the body cavity. To make this easier, form a 'V' with the first two fingers of your left hand (for a right-handed person) and place your fingers in the opening. Use your fingers to lift skin away from the intestines as you cut towards the breastbone holding the knife edge up.

Roll out the intestines and paunch, taking care to avoid breaking the bladder or tearing the intestines. Grab the intestines and urethra (penis you inserted into hole previously) below the bladder and squeeze closed. Gently pull these through the pelvis. Most of the remaining viscera will easily fall and pull away from the body cavity.

Cut the diaphragm (the muscle between chest and abdomen) away from the chest wall. Reach into the throat and cut the windpipe, gullet, and blood vessels. Pull the lungs and heart from the carcass.

Remove any remaining viscera and blood from the body cavity and wipe the cavity dry if possible.

Assist the cooling process by splitting the chest and propping the body cavity open with a stick. Don't yet split the aitch (pelvis) bone if

you're dragging the carcass out. Spread the back legs apart to cool (they will be partially separated anyway). Move the carcass to the shade and keep it off the ground if possible.

Caping

Caping is necessary to help prevent hair slippage and abrasion. Some hunters are uncomfortable with fully caping a deer, but can at least partially cape the animal. Although the taxidermist can repair small cuts in the hide that may be made during caping, hair slippage and damage are not repairable. The method described here is for partial caping in the field for transporting the cape and head to camp where caping is more conveniently completed. If in doubt, leave extra tissue as you or the taxidermist can remove it later.

Partial Caping

Cut through the hide around the circumference of the deer's body about four inches behind the front legs.

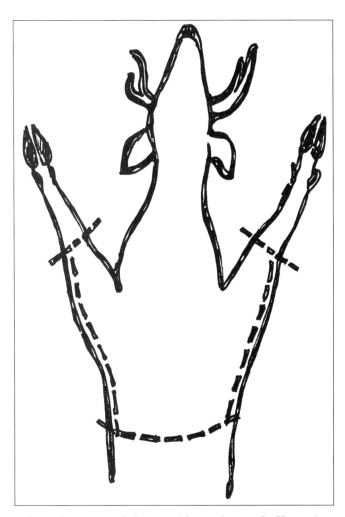

Cuts for a partial cape (deer shown belly up).

Cut the hide around each front leg just above the knee, then cut along the back of the legs to meet the cut around the body.

Skin legs and body, working toward the head, as far as possible.

Roll the "tube" of skin up under the chin and antlers and tie in place with string.

Saw through the neck as close as possible to the head.

Transport the head and cape to camp and finish caping as soon as possible, or immediately take the partial cape to a taxidermist.

Completing the Cape

Unroll the skin. Cut the hide up the back along the midline to the back of the skull plate, then make short cuts at 45° angles to the base of each antler.

Pry and lever the skin from the antler bases using a blunt tool like a screwdriver. Take care to get all the hair, but do not cut.

Skin the hide over and around the head, cutting through the base of the ears.

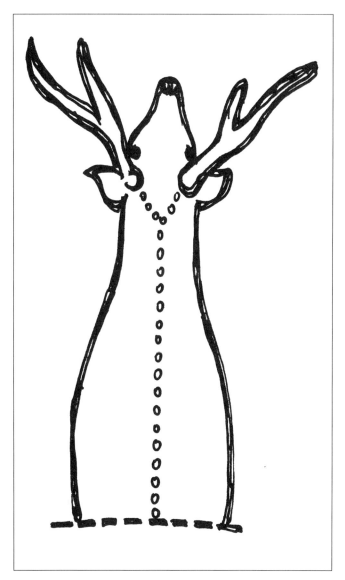

To complete the cape, add these cuts to the partial-cape cuts indicated previously (deer shown from top).

Use special care around the eyes as eyelids are difficult to repair. Carefully scoop out with your knife the tear glands found in the lower front corner of each eye.

Cut along the gumline to release the upper and lower lips, then finish skinning the head.

Split the gums from the inside and turn open to expose the soft tissue inside.

Skin the ears, turning inside-out as you go. Use a small, sharp knife or scalpel to free the skin as you go. WARNING: The skin is delicate here, so do not use excessive force. The farther you proceed toward the tip, the more delicate the skin becomes and the more chance of cutting and tearing the skin.

Cut away any remaining flesh on the cape and coat the flesh side of the hide with non-iodized salt, taking special care work salt into the lips and any areas where flesh may still cling to the skin. Use non-iodized salt because iodized salt will discolor the hide. Put the cape in the shade until you are ready to transport it. Roll the cape, nose first and hair out, and tie closed for transport.

Remove the antlers from the skull. Saw from a point just above the eye sockets to about two inches below the base of the antlers. Saw from the back of the skull to intersect with the first cut. Lift the antlers and skull plate from the rest of the skull and clean off all brain tissue and as much soft tissue as possible. For a taxidermist's convenience, cut through the eye sockets horizontally through to the base of the skull as another option.

Saw cuts for removing antlers.

Most any tree will do when you need to skin a deer in the field ...

Skinning

Skinning is most easily done while the deer is hanging, either from the neck or from the hind legs. But in the field, it often must be done on the ground as described here. Skinning methods are similar in all cases.

Always cut the hide from underneath the skin, that is from the inside out. In this way you do not cut hair, which dulls your knife and contaminates the meat with cut hair. While skinning, firmly grip and pull the hide out from the carcass. Make all cuts holding the side of the knife blade parallel to the skin to avoid damaging the hide. And always skin so that the outside of the hide and hair fall away from the carcass as you go.

Skinning a Deer

See page 157 for an illustration of the cuts to make.

First, remove the forelegs below the knee and the hind legs below the hock by cutting at the break joints. Alternatively, just saw off the legs.

Cut the hide along the midline of the chest to the lower jaw, then around the neck.

Cut the hide from the midline cut out along the back of the front and rear legs.

Skin the legs from their lower portions toward the body. Let the outside of the hide and hair fall away from the carcass as you go.

Continue skinning the body towards the backbone. Continue to make sure that the outside of the hide and hair falls away from the carcass as you go.

Roll the carcass onto the clean, separated hide so that the carcass is lying on its side. Alternatively, roll it onto a lightweight plastic tarp. Finish skinning around the back to meet the freed skin from the other side.

If you want some prime buckskin, apply non-iodized salt to the flesh side of the hide to preserve it until it is tanned.

... and you'll want to take him out in pieces when you shoot him in the bottom of a canyon like this.

Save a Buck's Skin

After four soggy days of hunting and camping in the mountains of northern Utah, a shower and a nap back at my brother's rural Wellsville home felt great. I awoke refreshed and, lo and behold, the October sun had finally made an appearance. I'm not one to waste too much hunting time and, attitude adjusted, I loaded a rifle to take a walk in the willow and cottonwood bottoms of the Bear River behind his house.

The day practically sparkled with a washed blue sky above, yellow willow patches and golden cottonwoods lining the river, fresh fields of green alfalfa spilling into the river bends, and the snow-capped peaks of the Wasatch Front and the Wellsville Mountains surrounding it all. This soft, tame valley offered a beauty all its own, compared to the harsh, wild, foggy peaks I had been climbing.

The valley also harbors a resident population of mule deer, and I found my first ones in a half-acre patch of willows — a half dozen does and fawns that bounced through the river bottom grass to the next brushy thicket. I hunted a few more willow patches downriver, then crossed at a riffle and worked the other bank back upstream.

I climbed a small hillside and sat in the sun awhile, eating a sweet yellow apple from a tree in the ravine below and studying the cover ahead. As I stood up and began working my way down the slope, a deer scrambled out of a small willow patch below me and splashed across the river. Antlers, not much, but antlers nonetheless! I made the decision quickly. This would be some prime venison. The deer started running toward a patch of cottonwoods as the rifle came to my shoulder, swung ahead of him and touched off.

A hard-earned Utah buck, taken on a golden October day.

He dropped on the spot. Either my swing was a little too energetic or maybe he wasn't running as fast as I thought. The bullet caught him high in the neck. One of his small antlers was completely hidden in the deep cottonwood leaves when I trotted up to him. The sun was dropping behind the peaks of the Wellsvilles, and I dressed him in the orange glow of the warm Utah evening. A breeze rattled the cottonwood leaves still clinging above.

I saved the flawless skin of that beautiful little buck, had it tanned, and it now adorns a variety of antler mounts in my home. I've since had the skin of other bucks tanned too, for a variety of uses such as gloves, craft projects for the kids, buckskin moccasins, and I even put one to use as a chamois. Saving a buck's skin is a great way to relive a hunt many times over. It also allows you to make even greater use of the resource. Even if the deer isn't Boone and Crockett or Pope and Young material, give it a try sometime.

TJC

Quartering

Quartering can be done either with the hide on or off. Leaving the skin on helps prevent moisture loss and contamination by debris, but the resulting pieces of hide are generally too small for tanning. Here's how to quarter.

Remove the forelegs below the knee and the hind legs below the hock by cutting at the break joints. Alternatively saw off the legs.

Remove the head. (Cape the deer first if you want a shoulder mount!) Use a saw to cut through the neck or insert a knife through the atlas joint found between the base of the skull and the first neck vertebrate. If using a knife, don't cut straight through, but work the point around the natural curvature of the overlapping bones.

Separate the carcass behind the last rib. Use a knife to cut from the backbone to the tips of the ribs, then saw through the backbone. Cut and saw from inside the body cavity.

Split the front and back halves into quarters by sawing lengthwise through the backbone from inside the body cavity.

Boning

Boning is the most efficient way to transport meat from the field, and it is the best way to prepare the carcass for cutting and wrapping the deer yourself. The well-defined muscles of a deer make boning a simple chore, even for the novice. Use your fingers to separate the muscles as much as possible before cutting and, once cut and wrapped, boned meat requires no further cutting and trimming before cooking. (See the "Additional Care" section of this chapter for instructions on what to cut these boned pieces into.)

Remove the front leg from the carcass. While lifting the leg, cut along the ribs underneath the leg from the chest towards the backbone. Note that there is no "socket" connection between the body and leg here; just ligaments.

Remove the two large shoulder muscles from the scapula. Trim the remainder of the meat from the leg, neck, chest and between the ribs.

Remove the backstrap that runs along both sides of the backbone. Begin by cutting deep to the ribs along the vertical processes of the backbone from the base of the neck to the pelvis. At the base of the neck, make a second cut out from the backbone, perpendicular to the first cut. Now "peel" the backstrap from the carcass using your knife to free it from the ribs as necessary.

Remove the hind legs from the carcass. Begin your cut at the backbone and work along the hip bone and pelvis until you reach the ball and socket joint where the head of the femur joins the pelvis. Be patient as this is a tortuous path. Lift and move the leg to open the joint and expose the ligaments holding it in place. Cut the ligaments and remove the leg.

Remove the individual muscles from the rear legs.

Position the leg with its inside facing down and remove the top, or outside round, which comprises the upper, outside, rear portion of the leg.

Remove the rump portion.

Remove the bottom, or inside round, which is located just inside of the top round.

Remove the sirloin tip, which is a complex of four muscles located on the front of the leg.

Trim the meat from the shank portion of the leg.

Trim the flank meat from behind the ribs and remove the tenderloins from the inside of the body cavity.

Equipment For Field Care

The equipment listed below allows you to accomplish all the field care detailed in this chapter. Carry mandatory items during the hunt. The optional items are used in the field only when employing some of the alternatives for field care. Carry these items during the hunt at your discretion. The optional items should always be available at camp or your vehicle.

Mandatory Equipment

Knife. A knife is used for the cutting required during most field care chores. The style of knife and blade design are personal preference, although for field care there is no compelling reason for a blade greater than four inches long.

Rope. Keep 20 feet of rope in your pack for such things as tying deer to a tree while field dressing, dragging a carcass from the field and lashing deer quarters to a pack board.

Kitchen string. Several feet of kitchen string will make it easy to tie your tag to the animal, to tie the anus and urethra closed during field dressing, and to tie a partial cape in place.

Rags. Field dressing sometimes gets messy. Use clean rags after field dressing to wipe your hands and the inside of the carcass.

Flashlight. Sometimes you'll need extra light. Some of the field care is sure to occur after dark. A headlamp will keep your hands free and provide light were it is most needed.

Optional Equipment

Bone saw. If you'll be removing antlers and quartering the deer, you'll need a saw. Lightweight saws are available in folding and "Wyoming" styles.

Ceramic sticks or steel. A sharp knife makes the cutting easier and is less dangerous than a dull knife.

Plastic gloves. If you choose to wear gloves while field dressing to exclude any chance of contracting disease keep them with your mandatory equipment.

Game bag. A game bag will keep blow flies from the skinned carcass. This could be considered mandatory equipment in warm weather.

Block and tackle. A lone hunter can use this simple tool to hang a deer from a tree or load a large deer into the back of a truck.

Plastic sled. For dragging a deer from the field.

Nylon harness. Wear it for dragging a deer from the field. The type that is used over both shoulders simultaneously is preferred.

Wheeled deer carrier. If the terrain allows, these carts make quick work of hauling an intact carcass from the field.

Plastic sheet. A small plastic sheet provides a clean area for placing a skinned carcass on to work.

Packboard or backpack. A board or pack is used to transport quarters or boned meat from the field. Be sure they are large and sturdy enough for the job and have a waist belt so that most of the weight is carried on your hips.

Salt, 4 pounds, non-iodized. Spread on the cape and/or hide to dry and preserve it before tanning.

Screwdriver. To pry the skin from the antlers during caping.

Additional Care

Although cutting the meat and cooking are not field care techniques, we mention them here because poor meat handling and cooking can negate the results of excellent field care. It is a very simple chore to cut and wrap boned meat; it truly is a job any hunter can do. Described below are the recommended cuts from the various boned muscles you'll end up with.

Mule deer venison is highly esteemed.When cared for and then prepared properly it is a real treat on the table. We find it as good as any

whitetail. Mule deer venison just seems to have a mild twang all its own. Maybe it's a hint of sage or chaparral or quaky buds or snowberries that adds the flavor of the wild, Western habitat the deer came from.

More recently, venison is becoming prized by the health-conscious who desire meat that is very low in fat. Venison is the Holy Grail of the gourmet, and has graced the world's finest tables throughout the ages. Here's how to finish the preparations for making it ready to grace yours as well.

Cuts From The Boned Meat

Trim all excess connective tissue from the meat and cut into pieces that are ready to cook. Wrap the cuts in meal-size portions using plastic-coated freezer paper to prevent the dehydration that causes freezer burn. To promote quick freezing, do not stack the packages too deep in the freezer. If you have access, it might be worth a quick, hard freeze at a powerful freezer in a real locker plant, if a nearby facility offers such services. It's worth inquiring.

Frozen venison will maintain its quality for up to nine months. Thaw the meat in the refrigerator, not at room temperature.

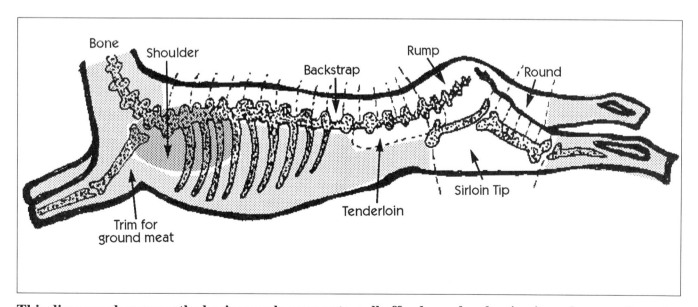

This diagram shows you the basic muscle groups to pull off a deer when boning it, and names the cuts.

First, cut the shoulder muscles into 3/4-inch cubes for use as stew meat or for grinding.

Grind the meat that was trimmed from the shanks. Shank trim makes serviceable meat for sausage, although better sausage will be obtained if an equal amount of whole muscle meat is also included.

Slice the backstrap into 3/4-inch thick chops. Larger chops are obtained by slicing into "butterfly chops." To butterfly the backstrap, only cut three fourths of the way through the muscle on every other slice. Open these double-chops as a butterfly would spread its wings, effectively doubling the cross sectional area of your loin chops.

Slice the top and inside rounds into 3/4-inch thick steaks or cut these into stew meat.

Slice the rump into thin strips for fajitas and stir fry, or cut the rump into 1" cubes for kabobs.

Leave the sirloin whole as this makes an excellent roast.

Leave the tenderloins whole, or cut into medallions for frying.

Cooking Venison

There are many excellent game cookbooks available and it is great fun to experiment using these as a starting point. For the less adventuresome, most recipes for beef work well with venison if several points are kept in mind:

Employ cooking methods appropriate to the cut of meat. In general, follow the guidelines recommended for the those same cuts of beef or pork. For example do not grill the tough shoulder cuts, but stew them. Conversely, do not slight the natural tenderness of the backstrap by stewing it. Grill the chops (medallions or butterfly) and enjoy the flavors that develop!

Do not overcook venison. Venison is naturally low in fat which decreases its juiciness. Venison's tendency towards dryness is compounded as the meat is cooked to greater internal temperatures. From a health standpoint, it is adequate to cook whole muscle cuts to an internal temperature of 150°F (medium rare

doneness). So yes, you can enjoy that venison chop before it is charred through; in fact, that may be the ONLY way to enjoy it. Ground venison should be cooked to an internal temperature of 160°F.

The alternative venison cooking strategy is "slow and moist." For instance, you can create soups, stews, chili, Swiss steak, stroganoff, barbecue, tacos, etc. This strategy moistens and tenderizes the meat through cooking for relatively long periods, in liquid.

To quote an old song, when cooking venison you've got to accentuate the positive (keep the flavor in by not overcooking) or eliminate the negative (cook it slowly with moisture which avoids dryness/toughness), and don't mess with anything in between!

A Just Reward

There is no denying it. Field care of mule deer – especially the big ones which choose to live, and hence get harvested, far from roads – is a chore. Field dressing is by nature a bit messy. Skinning and caping are tedious. Transport involves hard physical labor.

Consequently, field care may not ever be the stuff of fond memories. The other parts of the hunt—the country, the stalk, the shot, the camaraderie— all that can be looked back upon with smiles, but field care is no less a part of the hunt, and the hunt is not complete until field care is complete. The best field care requires planning and preparation. The rewards of conscientious field care are excellent venison for the table and a mount by which to remember the hunt for years to come. Along with the memories, those two items make the trip worth every ounce of effort.

My Mountain

The Utah mountain was mine alone as I approached the bowl that was once a glacial cirque. The depression has since been pioneered by four-foot tall chaparral. I had struggled to this point over the last six hours, gaining several thousand feet in elevation from where I had parked my truck at the edge of this newly-designated wilderness area.

No vehicles are allowed in wilderness areas, and in many cases that is all that keeps them out. On this mountain, however, the brush and the rough, steep terrain have always kept them out.

The mountain's peak formed an impressive backdrop, rising yet another thousand feet above me. My destination was a meadow at the top of the bowl, another hour's hike. Thankfully it was at the same elevation. I sat on some rocks to rest and removed my pack, which contained the necessities for a 3-day stay on the mountain, including the tools to care for a trophy deer and its meat in the wilderness. The September sun was warm but the breeze began to cool me off.

I glassed the bowl and then, for fun, my house in the valley far below. After a few minutes, two mule deer appeared. Both were four-pointers with spreads in the 20-inch range, typical of the 2 1/2-year-old bucks on this mountain who are smart or lucky enough to have escaped the regular-season hunting pressure of their first antlered year. As I watched the pair feed, another buck emerged from the chaparral, and then another. Both were four-pointers, a little larger than the previous ones, but I was looking for something bigger on this hunt.

I had drawn a tag for a special mid-September high-country hunt held well before Utah's regular late-October rifle season. Believing this was a real opportunity to take a nice buck, I was trying for one for the wall. I had already explored my options for a mount, and was prepared to care for a cape in the field. I was also prepared to care for the meat, a chore I had become very familiar with on previous hunts on this mountain. But this time I was higher up and the weather was warmer than ever before.

Special care would have to be taken with any deer I harvested and I was ready to cape, field dress and skin any buck immediately. This was especially important since the warm September days were, as of late, compounded by cloud cover and rain that kept things from cooling off at night.

Just as I stood up to leave in search of bigger bucks, one appeared out of nowhere. I quickly sank back down and studied this one carefully. He was in the 26-inch class, with four points on a high, thick rack. This was by far the best buck I had ever seen on this mountain. He could have been the Daddy of the first two bucks I had spotted. I decided to try for him if he distanced himself from the group and presented a safe shot.

But then the wind swirled and the deer must have gotten a whiff of human scent in their isolated summer stronghold. The bucks began to trot off in close file, the largest one pulling up the rear. They ate up the ground fast, and in no time disappeared into my side of a gully, about 250 yards away. I readied for a shot, hoping the buck would pause coming out of the gully before disappearing again into the chaparral beyond.

After a minute they began climbing out, one-by-one at the place I had hoped, but none paused before disappearing into the sea of green. Miraculously though, the fifth buck stopped! It was obviously a buck but was it my big one? My thoughts flashed back to the my previous three days on the other side of this mountain, hunting in the clouds and a constant drizzle, seeing only two tiny bucks. The Western sky was again clouding up.

At the shot, the buck lunged forward, then slipped and slid into the gully. After reaching the spot, it took me 15 more minutes to find him, 50 yards down, wedged against the only living thing in the rockslide, a small sapling in a small bit of soil caught among the rocks and boulders. Eons of runoff had washed the boulders into this gully. It was small at its start here in the high country, but opened into the biggest canyon of the mountain, with maple brush and then wheat fields many miles below.

I marveled for a few moments at the buck's sleek beauty. He was so fat the bullet holes, entering at the top of the near-side ribs and exiting below the far-side front leg, had both sealed shut. There was no blood trail to him.

But it was not the buck I thought. Had the deer switched order in the gully before exiting on the far side? Or had I overestimated the size of the rack?

Somehow, it didn't matter. The quality was in the hunt itself, in this place, and in the quiet. Anyway, he was the biggest mule deer buck I had shot up to that point and he was beautiful.

The mountain was mine alone as I began my work in the warm September sun, thunderheads breaking over the peaks above.

CEC

Special thanks to Charles E. Carpenter of Wellsville, UT for pulling together the "meat" of this chapter.

Chapter 11

Mule Deer State-by-State

Introduction

This chapter goes hand-in-hand with the next chapter, Planning the Hunt. As you'll see, the necessary first step to planning any mule deer hunt is selecting a state in which to hunt. So here is the information you need to get on the trail to making that decision.

If you hunt muleys already and want to expand your horizons, you'll value what you find in the pages that follow.

Now for many of the states profiled like Colorado, Wyoming, Montana, Utah, Idaho and New Mexico, an entire book could be written about each one's mule deer history, herds and management. Much of that information is available directly from the states

themselves if you're interested – and it is interesting stuff.

Here we'll concentrate instead on the present state of the herds, how seasons run, how licenses are allocated, where some of the better mule deer areas are, the public and private land situation in that state, and where you can get more information.

Of course, mule deer herds are dynamic, changing with the harshness of the seasons, their habitat, and the hunting pressure game departments allow. But what follows will form your basis for beginning to decide where, when and how you'll hunt. Chapter 12, Planning the Hunt, helps you complete the picture.

Arizona

Mule Deer Habitat, Herds and Harvest.

"Mule deer are found throughout Arizona, from sea level to 13,000 feet in elevation," said Ray Lee of the Arizona Game and Fish Department. "In general, at the lower elevations and in the southern half of the state, you'll find the desert race of mule deer. In the northern half of the state, principally north of the Mogollon Rim, it's all the Rocky Mountain variety of mule deer."

Erase any image of Arizona as all desert. There's a good variety of mule deer habitat out there, from Ponderosa Pine foothills to sagebrush plateaus to aspen/fir forest in some of the mountain ranges. Arizona has about 120,000 mule deer, and the harvest hovers around 12,000 deer a year.

Mule Deer Seasons.

Archery season in Arizona runs from the latter part of August through September, and then again from December through January. Rifle seasons traditionally run from the last Friday in October through November.

Licenses and Allocation.

Arizona has some general rifle hunts with over-the-counter licenses available, but many of the most interesting units, the ones with big buck potential, have a computer drawing for tags.

"Nonresidents are not limited in the general license units, or south of the Colorado River," said Lee. "But nonresidents are limited to no more than 10% of the buck permits north of the river. But typically, only about 3% of the draw goes to nonresidents anyway."

Nonresidents pay $78.50 for a license plus $85.50 for a tag; residents pay $18.00 plus $17.50, respectively. Archery permits are over-the-counter, and some muzzleloader-only hunts are available through a drawing.

Top Mule Deer Areas.

"The oak brush types of habitats you'll find at the 5,000- to 6,000-foot elevation in Arizona will typically support the highest densities of mule deer," Lee said.

For big bucks, the classic Kaibab range still cannot be beat. On the other hand, Lee said, "There are some very old and big bucks out in the deserts. You have to be tough and patient to hunt them. There aren't tons of deer out there. But you'll likely be alone, hunting one-on-one, and you could find the buck of a lifetime."

Public and Private Land.

It doesn't get much better than Arizona for finding public land to hunt.

"Eighty percent of Arizona is public land," Lee said.

There are huge chunks of BLM land in Arizona, as well as several national forests, and a surprising amount of state land. As for private land, the situation in Arizona is relatively good. Access fees are still relatively uncommon here, and reasonable requests from responsible-looking and sounding hunters are often met with permission to hunt. Arizona also has several hunter access programs to maintain and improve hunter/rancher relationships.

Although not generally thought of as a top mule deer destination for hunters, Arizona is a true sleeper with lots of public land and good access, decent opportunities for nonresidents, some big bucks, low or controlled hunter pressure, and even some relatively mild weather during the rifle seasons.

For more information contact:

Arizona Game and Fish Department
2221 West Greenway Road
Phoenix, AZ 85023
602-942-3000

California

Mule Deer Habitat, Herds and Harvest.

When you think of California don't think of the big cities, palm trees and traffic jams. Instead, turn your eyes eastward to the High Sierras, then down their easten slope and into the true inter-mountain West. There's plenty of it in California, and plenty of mule deer in the state's deer herd of 700,000 animals. True, many of the deer in that total are blacktails but there are enough Rocky Mountain muleys in the north, and desert muleys in the south, to please any hunter. Recently, about 50,000 hunters per year have been bringing home venison.

Mule Deer Seasons.

Take a map of the U.S. and cut out California. If you set it on the east coast, California would stretch from New England to Georgia, and go inland at least a state's worth to boot! That's a lot of country, and California's deer seasons reflect that diversity. Some blacktail rifle seasons start in August, but the "X" zones where mule deer live generally open the first week of October, or a week either side of it. Archery on the coast starts as early as July, and muzzleloaders have 10 or so special hunts around the state.

Licenses and Allocation.

For the higher-demand "X" zones, there is a random drawing, with no differentiation between residents and nonresidents for tags; these applications are usually due in early June, with a drawing in early July. Most of the other zones, which routinely don't sell out of their tag allotment, sell tags over-the-counter. Obtain an application from Fish and Game first, then send it to a regional office or the de-partment's Licensing and Revenue Division. Nonresidents pay $94.75 for the license and $162.50 for the deer tag; residents pay $27.05 plus $17.85 for the tag.

Top Mule Deer Areas.

We'll concentrate on true mule deer, not the state's great blacktails, which are an addiction all their own.

"For Rocky Mountain mule deer, the area east of Interstate 5 north to Tahoe is great coun-try," said Russ Mohr of the California Depart-ment of Fish and Game. "This is where you'll find the biggest bucks, too. From there, go down the east side of the Sierras to find our in-teresting subspecies, the California mule deer, which results from an interbreeding of black-tails and muleys and the desert mule deer (called burro deer here) of the Southeast."

When you look at the regulations, look at the "X" zones of the north and east. "But don't overlook the desert zones," said Mohr. "There are some nice bucks there, too. But get some advice from the locals on how to hunt!"

Public and Private Land.

In general in California, you move toward public lands as you get higher and see more timber.

"There is a lot of Forest Service and BLM land in the state," said Mohr. He also points out California's Private Land Management Program, which allocates tags to landowners for sale. These hunts are fairly expensive be-cause the landowners are dealing with fairly high demand for what are some great hunts, but you can get some really nice bucks. The central and southern areas of the state see the highest proportions of private land.

For more information contact:

California Department of Fish and Game
1416 9th Street
Sacramento, CA 95814
916-653-7664

Colorado

Mule Deer Habitat, Herds and Harvest.

Colorado is probably king when it comes to mule deer states, both in terms of sheer numbers (800,000 deer, mostly muleys) and big bucks. Just look at the mule deer section of Boone and Crockett, Pope and Young or any other record book.

"We have everything from flatland sage-brush to 14,000-foot peaks and everything in between — pines and quakies, piñon-juniper hills, oak brush plateaus, high-plains and true prairie. There are mule deer at some density in all of it," said Brad Frano of the Colorado Division of Wildlife.

Colorado's annual harvest runs in the neighborhood of 55,000 to 60,000 deer; again, these are almost all muleys.

Mule Deer Seasons.

Archery season runs during the month of September. There are three rifle seasons; a five-day season at the beginning of October, an 11-day season in the latter part of October and a nine-day season in early November. Actual hunts vary by region and unit, so get the Big Game Hunter's Information Package mentioned at the end of this section. Muzzleloaders (by permit draw) take to the plains, prairies hills and mountains in mid-September.

Licenses and Allocation.

West of Interstate 25, general rifle seasons are the norm, with licenses available over-the-counter. This is good because you can always hunt, but it also causes fairly high hunter pressure. There are some limited-draw units here, with applications due in March.

East of I-25, every unit has a draw, simply because the habitat is so accessible and deer numbers are relatively limited. Colorado has a preference point system.

"Sooner or later you'll draw a tag for the hunt you really want," said Frano. Most of the state offers over-the-counter archery licenses, but there are some special-draw units. A small muzzle-loader hunt (8,000 tags) is administered by draw per unit.

There are two pluses to Colorado's system. Nonresidents aren't discriminated against in any of the draws and Colorado is one of the last states to offer general, over-the-counter rifle hunting licenses. The drawback to the latter is that during those rifle seasons you have to be willing to work to get off the beaten path, away from any crowds.

Nonresidents pay $150.25 for a Colorado deer license, residents $20.

Top Mule Deer Areas.

With all of Colorado's great mule deer habitat, how does one focus in on the best areas to hunt? For the highest densities of mule deer, which may also mean fairly high densities of hunters unless you get into the boondocks, look to The White River National Forest, the Bear's Ear Herd of the Routt National Forest, the Grand Mesa National Forest and the San Juan National Forest.

Where are the big ones? Frano said, "Look to the state's far northwest corner and the Little Snake Herd, then work your way south from there into the high plateau country of oak brush pockets and sage."

Frano also pointed out some other areas with high buck:doe ratios, which usually means there are some big bucks in the population. These include the Bijou Creek, Big Sandy, Chico Basin and Arkansas River herds.

Public and Private Land.

"West of Interstate 25, public access is great" says Frano. "Thirteen National Forests cover 30% of the state's land mass, and there are millions of acres of BLM land. You may have to do some mapwork and footwork to get access to some of the BLM land, but it's there. Many state trust lands and wildlife areas top it all off." Simply put, there is great mule deer hunting, and a lot of room to do it, in Colorado.

The situation is different east of I-25, (prairie and high plains country). Here almost all the land is private.

"You need to line up access long before you even apply for a hunt here," said Frano. "More and more, the better land out there is being tied up by outfitters and those charging trespass fees. There are fewer and fewer places you can hunt on a handshake, unless you're looking for does. The landowners are very protective of their buck mule deer."

But this also means there are some really big bucks out on those plains. These deer are worth some work to get access. And you can have an effective hunt without an outfitter. Of course, for the right money with the right outfitter, you can have the hunt of a lifetime.

For more information contact:

Colorado Division of Wildlife
6060 Broadway
Denver, CO 80216
303-297-1192

Note: Be sure to call or write for Colorado's Big Game Hunting Information Package. It's about as complete a resource as you'll find, and is full of interesting and pertinent information on planning a Colorado hunt.

Idaho

Mule Deer Habitat, Herds and Harvest.

Mule deer inhabit every county of Idaho. In addition, Idaho offers almost every type of mule deer habitat, from classic foothill/mountain areas of aspen and lodgepole, to sage flatlands, grasslands, true desert and agricultural areas. So the big question becomes, where do I go to find one of the estimated 160,000 mule deer that live here? Idaho is just a good mule deer state, from the classic southeastern corner to the steep and remote Salmon River country to the high-and-dry southwest. Idaho sees a harvest of around 40,000 to 50,000 deer a year, some of them whitetails.

Mule Deer Seasons.

The archery season generally runs the first three weeks of September. Rifle and muzzle-loader seasons vary widely from unit to unit, so your best bet here is to get a copy of the state's hunting regulations. October is the month when most of these seasons are held. There are a few late-season opportunities as well.

Licenses and Allocation.

Idaho is somewhat unique among the prime mule deer states in that it allocates licenses on a first-come, first-served basis rather than a drawing. Planning is the key. With an application acceptance date beginning December 1 for the following year's seasons, you have to make your hunting plans, including unit, specific land you'll hunt and general timing, almost a full year in advance. And because it's first-come, first-served, you're well advised to apply right on December 1 because some units, especially those in the popular big-buck country of the southeast, sell out quickly. Note that applications are accepted beginning December 1, not before, so time things right.

A nonresident mule deer license costs $101.50 and a tag is $226.50, for a $300+ total that is near the top of the West's scale. Residents pay $7.50 plus $16.50 for the tag. All archers and muzzleloaders need to add a $9.00 stamp to their license.

Top Mule Deer Areas.

Southeastern Idaho is renowned big buck country, and continues to be as good a bet as anywhere. The rugged Salmon River country is also excellent, producing big bucks by giving them enough space and terrain to grow old. This is big country with fairly low deer densities. That keeps hunter pressure down compared to the more popular areas. For sheer fun and a unique experience, try hunting the wide-open southwestern part of Idaho. This is dry, high-desert country that supports a surprising number of deer. Some good bucks can be had if you're patient and don't take the first one that comes along.

Public and Private Land.

"Two-thirds of Idaho is public land, so access is excellent," said Lonn Kuch of the Idaho Department of Fish and Game. "Plus, most of the prime mule deer country is right there on public land, so there's really no need to go to private land to hunt, if you don't want to. There's so much good public land, it doesn't matter."

This is good news for a mule deer hunter traveling to Idaho, and it's what makes Idaho such a great place. Still, for those wanting to hunt on private land, access is available and fee hunting is becoming more and more common on the ranches and farmlands.

For more information contact:

Idaho Fish and Game Department
600 S. Walnut, Box 25
Boise, ID 83707
208-334-3700

Kansas

Mule Deer Habitat, Herds and Harvest.

The western third of Kansas is considered mule deer country. You'll find the deer right out on that open range, particularly in the higher elevation grasslands. Mule deer make up about a third of the state's deer harvest, which has been hovering around 50,000 animals per season.

Mule Deer Seasons.

Kansas' rifle season starts on the first Wednesday in December and lasts for 12 days. Bowhunters can take to the range from October 1 to December 31, except during the rifle season. Muzzleloaders get two chances. There's a special early hunt held in late September and muzzleloaders are legal during the general rifle season.

Licenses and Allocation.

Like other prairie regions, Kansas has to limit the number of mule deer permits to control the harvest. Both resident and nonresident mule deer hunters must apply by May 31 for a firearms license in one of Kansas' 18 deer management units. Nonresidents are allocated a portion of the permits. Permits are specific to both species (whitetail or mule deer) and sex (buck or doe/antlerless). Archery licenses are not limited, and can be purchased directly from the Department of Wildlife and Parks, or from vendors. A nonresident hunting license costs $65.50, plus a $205.50 charge for a buck permit. Residents have a $15 license plus a $30.00 buck permit. Doe permits are also sometimes available in certain units, for additional permit fees.

Top Mule Deer Areas.

"Everywhere in the western third of the state has decent mule deer populations, and some good bucks," said Bob Mathews of the Kansas Department of Wildlife and Parks.

Public and Private Land.

"The hunting is good, and you can find some big bucks," said Mathews. "But your first challenge is going to be finding a place to hunt."

There is little public hunting land in Kansas, but the private-land situation is "pretty good", according to Mathews.

"The landowners are generous if you ask permission to hunt, and you are respectful. Most will allow deer hunting, as well as hunting for other game, often without a fee," he said. "The key is working hard at locating a spot in advance, being polite, then treating the land as if it were your own. Good rules for anywhere."

For more information contact:

Kansas Department of Wildlife and Parks
512 SE 25th Ave.
Pratt, KS 67124
316-672-5911

Montana

Mule Deer Habitat, Herds And Harvest.

It's hard to say which mule deer state is best, but in terms of quality of hunting and chances for a good buck, Montana is definitely among the top contenders. Habitat is one reason. Mule deer are found throughout Montana, from the prairies in the east, through the Missouri River breaks, to the seemingly endless mountain ranges rising up from the central valley floors. Although Montana doesn't estimate how many mule deer are in the state, the harvest hovers around 50,000 animals, which is down from highs in the 90,000 range a decade ago. Still, that's a lot of mule deer.

Mule Deer Seasons.

Montana is divided into hunting regions. The rifle season varies slightly but in general runs for five weeks starting in late October, running through the Sunday after Thanksgiving

"We're definitely the most liberal state as far as allowing hunting during the rut," said Glenn Erickson of the Montana Department of Fish, Wildlife and Parks.

Serious buck hunters take note. Hunting big, old bucks during the rut (usually mid-November) can be a glorious thing, especially with the bucks accessible and out-and-about with the does. Bowhunters generally start the Saturday nearest September 1, stopping the week before rifle season starts. Muzzleloaders are free to hunt during regular rifle seasons, but have no special season allotted.

Montana is one of the few states where you can hunt mule deer bucks during the rut. The game plan then is simple: find the does and the bucks will not be far behind.

Licenses and Allocation.

Nonresidents, whether they hunt with rifle, muzzleloader or bow, must apply for and receive either a Big Game Combo license or a Deer Combo license to hunt. Each of these categories are allocated a certain number of licenses, and a hunter can go for an $835 outfitter tag or a $475 regular tag on the Big Game Combo. There is also a $675 outfitter tag or a $245 regular tag on the Deer Combo. Of course, the outfitter tags are to serve Montana's important outfitting industry, and all the prices are set yearly by the legislature, so they could change. Write Fish and Wildlife for application information; applications are usually due late winter.

Top Mule Deer Areas.

"The highest mule deer densities occur in the eastern, the far southwestern and central mountain regions," said Erickson. "Many of the biggest bucks, however, come from the high-plains northwestern country where whitetails are king but a few mule deer survive to grow big racks. Custer, Lincoln, Valley and Madison counties top the trophy lists as far as sheer numbers go."

Public and Private Land.

The western half of Montana has plenty of public land to roam, between all the national forests and BLM land. The eastern part – classic ranching country – is mostly private, especially the great southeastern country.

However, Montana has a Block Management Program for hunter access. In the program, a block of ranchers open their land to public hunting, under the control and patrol of the Fish, Wildlife and Parks Department. The landowners receive payment from the department, and in return get many hunter management problems off their backs. Contact Fish and Wildlife for details when you get applications.

"It's opening more and more land, and becoming very popular among landowners and sportsmen," said Erickson.

For more information contact

Montana Department of Fish,
   Wildlife and Parks
1420 E. Sixth Ave.
Helena, MT 59620
406-444-2535

Nebraska

Mule Deer Habitat, Herds and Harvest.

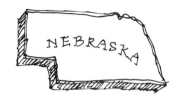

Nebraska's western half is the state's primary mule deer range. The muleys frequent the more open habitat, shying away from taking up residence in the wooded stream bottoms where the whitetails are moving in. The other part of the mule deer equation in Nebraska is finding rough country. In general, the rougher the better. Look for canyon-country, badland areas, any and all places with harsh terrain. Although not a premier mule deer state, Nebraska still harbors a fairly steady population of about 50,000 mule deer, and offers an annual mule deer harvest of about 10,000 animals. Fairly heavy hunting pressure and relatively easy terrain keep most bucks from growing to trophy status.

Mule Deer Seasons.

Archery season traditionally runs from September 15 through December 31, closing during the 9-day rifle season that begins on the second Saturday in November. Muzzleloaders take to the prairies and breaks on the first Saturday in December, for 16 days.

Licenses and Allocation.

Nonresidents can hunt muleys in Nebraska, which is good news. A license costs $150. Residents pay $22.25. Everyone has to buy a $10 habitat stamp. Archery and muzzleloader tags are unlimited for residents and nonresidents. Write or call Game and Parks for outlet information. Rifle tags are issued through a drawing. Believe it or not, nonresidents can draw rifle tags in Nebraska, although traditionally not in the prime units such as Frenchman.

Top Mule Deer Areas.

The Pine Ridge area offers the highest density of mule deer in the state. The more traditional wooded cover is the draw for both deer and hunters. The Frenchman unit is probably the best unit for overall mule deer numbers and trophy potential, although residents garner all the rifle tags here. Stick to the western part of the state for mule deer.

Public and Private Land.

Nebraska offers little public land relative to the premier mule deer states, but don't let that discourage you. Access can be had if you're willing to do a little letter writing and phone work. Nebraska is a friendly state.

"Nearly all landowners allow some hunting" said Karl Menzel of the Game and Parks Commission. Menzel said only about 7% of residents, and probably a few more nonresidents, pay a fee to hunt; that's pretty good in this day and age.

"The biggest challenge is getting an idea of where to go," said Menzel, "since Game and Parks doesn't give out landowner names unless landowners request it."

See chapter 12 for some ideas on finding out who to ask. You'll find about 200,000 acres of Forest Service and state land in the Pine Ridge unit. There are also about a million BLM acres in the state but access is landowner controlled.

A suggestion. Don't overlook Nebraska for a good archery hunt. Decent mule deer numbers, in the right areas, coupled with low archery pressure on private land make for a good opportunity. You may not bring home a monster, but your chances for having a good hunt and getting a nice buck are excellent.

For more information contact:

Nebraska Game and Parks Commission
2000 N. 33rd St. - P.O. Box 30370
Lincoln, NE 68503-0370
402-471-0641

Nevada

Mule Deer Habitat, Herds and Harvest

"Nevada is a great basin, and most of the water that falls here doesn't go to the sea," said Mike Hess of the Nevada Division of Wildlife. "The floor of that basin is at about 4,000 feet elevation, and we have about 100 mountain ranges, some of them very rugged, rising above that floor. You'll find Nevada's mule deer in those mountain ranges, from the foothills all the way up to the highest peaks."

Hess calls these mountain ranges "islands of habitat." About 10% of the state is considered mule deer habitat. Some of it is very good country, and you'll find deer from the piñon-juniper hills all the way up through classic aspen/lodgepole forests, to the deer's beloved bitterbrush. About 130,000 mule deer, mostly of the Rocky Mountain variety, live in Nevada. Harvest figures have been hovering at about 10,000 to 12,000 deer per year. Hunter success rates, in the rifle seasons, run between 40 percent and 60 percent each year.

Mule Deer Seasons

Archery season traditionally runs from the second Saturday of August through the first week of September. Rifle season opens the first Saturday in October and runs for four weeks. Muzzleloader hunters have two weeks to themselves between the archery and rifle seasons.

Licenses and Allocation.

Nonresidents can hunt Nevada, and can win up to 10% of the tags given out in a random computerized drawing. All permits—archery, rifle and muzzleloader—are given out via lottery, and are issued for specific management units. With a bonus point system in place, you earn credits to get preference in future draws. This is important considering the conservative harvest levels Nevada allows. But it's worth the wait for the quality of animal you'll find in the state. Estimates are that just one-half of the residents who apply get a permit in any given year.

Top Mule Deer Areas.

Nevada doesn't crop up in normal hunting conversation as a mule deer mecca, and that's good news for those who know about the state's potential.

"If you're highly motivated, put in your time and are willing to hunt fairly hard, you're likely to shoot a very good buck in Nevada," said Hess.

He attributes this to Nevada's very conservative hunt management, which leaves good numbers of deer on the range to winter, and plenty of bucks to grow old and get large racks.

"Of course, luck plays a factor, but for a real chance at a good, mature mule deer buck, you can't beat Nevada," said Hess. Every county in the state, save for one, has bucks in the Nevada record book. The bucks are out there.

Public and Private Land.

Nevada wins the public land sweepstakes with 87% of the state's surface area publicly owned. Remember, only about 10% of the state's acreage is considered mule deer habitat, but that only helps you know where the deer are going to be. Look for deer in the foothills and/or up on the slopes of the mountains, depending on the season. You might want to concentrate more on forest service land, versus BLM acreage, to find the better muley habitat. The person not familiar with the real Nevada will be surprised at the mountains and other good deer habitat the state holds. It's not just sand and desert.

For more information contact:
Nevada Division of Wildlife
P.O. Box 10678
Reno, NV 89520
702-688-1500

New Mexico

Mule Deer Habitat, Herds and Harvest.

New Mexico offers all the types of mule deer habitat anyone could want. There are seven zones in all, from true, flat desert through grasslands and then piñon-juniper hills and classic alpine habitat.

"You'll find desert muleys in the southern half of the state, and Rocky Mountain mule deer in the northern half," said Darryl Weybright, Big Game Project Leader for the New Mexico Department of Fish and Game. Weybright says an estimated 200,000 to 230,000 mule deer call New Mexico home, and hunters have recently been harvesting about 13,000 deer a year.

Mule Deer Seasons.

Rifle season timing varies by unit, but in general these hunts occur in November, and last from two to seven days. Archery season generally runs from September 1 to the 20, and hunters with muzzleloaders have the last 10 days of September to themselves. A license costs $180 for nonresidents, $23 for residents. There are some special higher-cost permits available for some high-demand units and some special low-pressure, high quality hunts.

Licenses and Allocation.

The popular northern quarter of the state has a drawing for licenses. Nonresidents are allo-

cated about 22% of the total. Half of that 22% is reserved for outfitters who can then resell the licenses to hunters. Many of these go at a substantial premium. The remainder of the state offers licenses over-the-counter, and they can be purchased up to the day before the season.

Top Mule Deer Areas.

"The highest mule deer densities occur in the southeastern mountain and desert regions," said Weybright. "But historically the north-central section of the state, with its Rocky Mountain subspecies bucks, produces the trophies."

Still, he says, hunting the desert mule deer is an experience all its own, and probably well worth a try for anyone who loves hunting muleys. You still can get a nice buck.

Public and Private Land.

"About 60% of New Mexico is public land. A good chunk of it is deer habitat. You can find a good place to hunt," says Weybright.

As for private land, Weybright said, "Ranches are realizing the income potential of their wildlife." That means trespass fees are becoming more and more common.

But access is available, often to some very good bucks and for a reasonable fee, for those willing to do their footwork. Meaning, see chapter 12 and get on the phone and your PC.

For more information contact:

New Mexico Department of
    Game and Fish
P.O. Box 25112
Santa Fe, NM 87504-5112
505-827-7911

North Dakota

Mule Deer Habitat, Herds and Harvest.

North Dakota mule deer are found mainly in the drainage of the Little Missouri River, but there are also scattered pockets of muleys throughout the state's western prairies. Generally, you'll find the mule deer in the rougher country – the badlands and breaks. Although North Dakota doesn't estimate the actual number of mule deer within its borders, the Game and Fish Department does survey units by flying over the state's primary mule deer habitat each spring and fall. This gives an idea of how the herds are doing and how successful reproduction was. Hunter success is good in North Dakota, running about 75% on mule deer bucks and 80% on does, in the rifle season. Harvest depends on how the herd is doing, but recent years have seen the take hovering around 2,500 to 3,000 muleys.

Mule Deer Seasons.

"By proclamation, all North Dakota big game seasons begin on a Friday at noon," said Bill Jensen of the North Dakota Game and Fish Department. "Bow season begins the last Friday in August and lasts through the end of the year. Rifle season starts the first Friday in November and runs 16 1/2 days, through the weekend before Thanksgiving. There are no special muzzleloader seasons for muleys, though hunters are welcome to use their muzzleloaders in the regular rifle season."

Licenses and Allocation.

Nonresidents can hunt mule deer in North Dakota, but the situation is very tight. In fact, it's usually fairly tight for residents as well. Mule deer rifle permits are awarded by unit through a drawing. Applications are due in mid-June.

"Nonresidents are eligible for 1% of the regular rifle season permits," said Jensen. "For rifle permits, we do have a preference point system for residents and nonresidents alike, but you have to apply every year to keep your points adding up."

The archery permit situation is not as tight. Apply for the state's "any deer" permit, which allows you to take a mule deer or a whitetail if you wish. The any deer archery permits are available on a first-come, first-served basis only from the department's Bismarck office. Nonresidents pay $155 for a deer license, residents $20.

Top Mule Deer Areas.

"Every year we see a few real nice mule deer bucks come out of North Dakota," said Jensen. "But we don't really manage for trophies. We manage the herd more to maximize the recreational opportunity the deer can provide."

You'll want to hit the rougher, broken-up country. That's where you'll find the mule deer anyway, and it's definitely the type of place where a buck can have a chance to live a few years and grow a good rack.

Public and Private Land.

"There are over a million acres of National Grasslands in North Dakota," said Jensen. "For the most part, there is pretty good access to these public lands. To hunt the badlands, an essential piece of equipment is the U.S. Forest Service's National Grasslands Map. For only $4 or so, it does two things of value. It shows you who owns what private land so you can attempt to get access if you want, and it shows many, though not all, of the roads."

This map is available from the Forest Service offices in Bismarck, Dickinson and Watford City. Call the regional Forest Service office, listed in chapter 12, for these numbers. As for private land access, some individuals charge an access fee and some don't, says Jensen.

For more information contact

North Dakota Game and Fish Department
100 N. Bismarck Expressway
Bismarck, ND 58501
701-328-6300

Oklahoma

Mule Deer Habitat, Herds and Harvest.

Oklahoma, which offers some prime white-tailed deer hunting, also offers mule deer in its panhandle region and the state's southwest corner. Estimates put Oklahoma's deer herd at about 350,000 animals, 3,000-5,000 of which are muleys.

"We see a few more taken every year," said Jerry Schaw of the Oklahoma Department of Wildlife Conservation. "The muleys seem to be doing okay here, and they're enough of a novelty that whitetail hunters like to take one when they see one."

Still, some hunters go to Oklahoma's western reaches specifically for its muleys.

"We don't differentiate between mule deer and whitetails in our harvest statistics," Schaw said.

Mule Deer Seasons.

Archery season runs from October 1 to the day before rifle season, which starts the Saturday before Thanksgiving and lasts through the Sunday after Thanksgiving. The late archery season then picks up and runs through the end of the year. Muzzleloaders have a special season, usually during the last week of October. Mule deer are fair game in all these seasons.

Licenses and Allocation.

As a nonresident you can hunt in Oklahoma if Oklahomans can hunt in your state. License are available over the counter, and cost $201 for a nonresident, $16.75 for a resident. There is no drawing except for a few controlled-access public hunting areas.

Top Mule Deer Areas.

The limited areas mentioned above hold all of Oklahoma's mule deer.

"Mostly, you'll find the muleys out in the rolling, grassy areas of sand dunes," said Schaw. Oklahoma is not known as a trophy state, but there are some lonely areas that allow a mule deer buck to grow a nice rack.

Public and Private Land.

"Oklahoma is about 97% privately held," said Schaw, "and the state seems to be turning more and more to leasing-type situations for hunting. Ranchers and farmers are realizing that wildlife pays as well as agricultural activities."

Still, he says, access can be had if you do your phone work and footwork, especially in the panhandle region where hunting rights are not as likely to be sealed up That's where most of the muleys are anyway. Don't overlook some of the areas where hunting rights may be leased by those only interested in the great quail hunting. Maybe you can get deer hunting access.

For more information contact:

Oklahoma Department of
    Wildlife Conservation
1801 N. Lincoln, P.O. Box 53465
Oklahoma City, OK 73152
405-521-3851

Oregon

Mule Deer Habitat, Herds and Harvest.

"Oregon offers a wide variety of mule deer habitat, from the classic type of mule deer country of the Snake River area, to heavily forested lodgepole forests, sage/juniper hills and the high desert of the southeast," said Tom Keegan of the Oregon Department of Fish and Wildlife.

Oregon traditionally winters over 200,000 mule deer. There are blacktails along the west slope of the Cascades and a few whitetails in some of the agricultural river valleys. About 25,000 muley bucks are harvested each year. Overall, hunters experience about a 35% success rate on mule deer.

Mule Deer Seasons.

Rifle season starts the Saturday closest to October 1 and runs for 12 days. Archery season generally runs for the five weeks prior to the rifle season, beginning the last or next-to-last weekend of August. Check the regulations for details on a few special muzzleloader seasons.

Licenses and Allocation.

"All of Oregon is under a draw/lottery process for the issue of rifle-hunting deer tags," said Keegan. "There are about 45 mule deer units in the state, and we have a preference point system so sooner or later you will get a tag for the hunt you want. Nonresidents can apply and hunt, but no more than 5% of the tags in any one unit can go to nonresidents."

Applications are due in mid-May. Of course, some units are more popular among hunters, so you'll wait longer for a tag there. Some of your better bets may be the areas with lower deer densities where competition for tags is less keen. There are also a few special muzzleloader hunts, usually under-subscribed, that are held during the rut period. The combination of limited hunting pressure and active bucks could be great as hunters have an almost guaranteed tag and a chance to hunt some big boys coming out of the hills for some breeding action. On the other hand, archery licenses and tags can be bought over-the-counter, except for a few special areas.

Nonresidents pay $53 for a hunting license and $176 for a tag, while residents pay $15 and $11, respectively. Note that in Oregon, you must buy the license outright before applying for the tag. That $53 license fee plus a $4 application fee is not refundable, even if you don't draw.

Top Mule Deer Areas.

"Oregon is a well-kept secret among mule deer states," said Keegan. "The Snake River country has high buck:doe ratios, which means older, bigger bucks are present, so does the southeast desert country."

There are also some dandy bucks in the central part of the state, but access to private land is sometimes a challenge here. If you're looking for high densities of deer, Keegan suggests you look along the east slope of the Cascades to central Oregon, and toward the Columbia River basin.

Public and Private Land.

"Oregon is predominantly a public-land state," said Keegan.

"The entire southeastern part of the state is probably 80% BLM land, and as you work your way up toward the northeast corner, you find a lot of U.S. Forest Service ground. Just get some good maps and look for the right colors. There is plenty of good public land to go hunting on."

As for private land, the situation is slowly turning toward a fee system as ranchers learn that wildlife can be a supplement to their income. The north central area of the state between the Columbia River and Blue Mountains is a primarily private land area where the hunting is good and fees for access are common.

For more information contact:

Oregon Department of Fish
    and Wildlife
2501 SW First Ave.
P.O. Box 59
Portland, OR 97207
503-872-5260

South Dakota

Mule Deer Habitat, Herds and Harvest.

South Dakota's mule deer live primarily west of the Missouri River, although the counties adjoining the river's east bank also harbor mule deer. Like the other prairie states, you'll find more mule deer in the badlands, breaks and higher elevations. The whitetails will be nearby, but they'll be in the brush and trees of the river and creek bottoms. In all, about 70,000 mule deer inhabit South Dakota (59,000 of them west of the Missouri), and hunters harvest around 12,000 per year. Most of this harvest comes from the West River units.

Mule Deer Seasons.

South Dakota's archery season runs from the last Saturday in September through the end of the year. Rifle seasons start at various times in November. The earliest season opens in the first week of November in the Black Hills; the West River season opens the second Saturday and the East River hunt begins the third Saturday. There are a few residents-only muzzleloader seasons, but only does can be taken.

Licenses and Allocation.

If you're a nonresident and want to hunt muleys with a rifle in South Dakota, your wait may be long. The state conducts a draw for all rifle tags, but in the mule deer country only 8% of the tags are allocated to nonresidents. Even some residents wait two, three or four years for tags they really want.

"As for archery hunting, licenses are not limited but you have to buy them either in person or by mail from the Game, Fish and Parks Department licensing office in Pierre," said spokesman Ken Moum. "So if you're a nonres-

ident doing it through the mail, give yourself plenty of time to get the applications, fill out and return them by mail, and get the licenses mailed back."

Residents pay $20 for any deer license, nonresidents $150.

Top Mule Deer Areas.

Although you can find some good mule deer in South Dakota, big bruisers are rare.

"Everything is just too accessible here – you can get to every nook and cranny in a truck," says Moum. "Most mule deer just don't get to grow that big and old."

Limited-access private lands would offer your best opportunities. Contact ranchers and outfitters in the southwest portion of the state.

Public and Private Land.

South Dakota is 85% private, so access can be tight. And, as with some other states, trespass fees are becoming more and more common. There are over a million acres of public land in the Black Hills, but almost all the deer taken there are whitetails. The big Indian reservations (Cheyenne River, Standing Rock, Rosebud, Lower Brule and Pine Ridge) have their own seasons and may be worth checking into. There are some limited opportunities on the national grasslands south and west of Pierre and in Perkins County in the northeast part of the state. But competition for the licenses offered in those units is stiff and hunting pressure can be heavy. Where does this all leave you as a nonresident, or even a resident? Look to get an archery tag and working the phone and back roads to get some early-season access in the ranchlands of the western part of the state.

For more information contact:

South Dakota Department of Game,
    Fish and Parks
523 E. Capitol
Pierre, SD 57501-3182
605-773-3387

Texas

Mule Deer Habitat, Herds and Harvest.

About 130,000 mule deer call Texas home. The majority (100,000) live in the Trans Pecos region of west Texas. The rest live in the panhandle. The Trans Pecos is a rugged area of mountains and basins, mostly desert shrub and grassland areas. The panhandle is more of a prairie environment. Though Texas is known for its whitetails, more than 17,000 hunters annually pursue muleys there. They bag between 3,000 and 4,000 of the big-eared deer per year.

Mule Deer Seasons.

In the Trans Pecos, the general rifle season traditionally starts the Saturday before Thanksgiving and runs for 16 days. The panhandle rifle season traditionally starts a week later, and likewise runs for 16 days. Archery season begins on the last Saturday in September and runs through October.

Licenses and Allocation.

Don't worry about a lottery in Texas. If you want to hunt mule deer in Texas, the license is available over-the-counter. Nonresidents pay $250 and get to shoot a turkey on this license, too. Residents pay $19.

Top Mule Deer Areas.

"The Trans Pecos region dominates Texas' mule deer harvest, with about 65% of the animals taken there. This is also where most of the dedicated mule deer hunting is done. Three other regions with mule deer; the rolling plains, high plains and Edwards plateau, split the balance of the harvest fairly evenly," said Mike Hobson of the Texas Parks and Wildlife Department. Hobson also pointed out that mule deer don't come easily there. The success rate for mule deer hunters is about 23 percent. There are about 70,000 hunter days devoted to mule deer each year.

Public and Private Land.

"Ninety-eight percent of Texas is privately owned," said Hobson. "You will have to deal with the landowner in order to secure a place to hunt. You can get access though."

Hobson suggests calling wildlife officers in the region, game wardens and chambers of commerce.

"There is land you can hunt but expect to work a bit to locate it, and to pay a fee to hunt," he said.

Fortunately for the Texas mule deer hunter, the lands his quarry call home are not generally as hospitable as the state's whitetail havens; hence, hunting access is sometimes easier and cheaper (which is a relative term).

For more information contact:

Texas Parks and Wildlife Department
4200 Smith School Road
Austin, TX 78744
800-792-1112 or 512-389-4800

Utah

Mule Deer Habitat, Herds and Harvest.

Utah is true mule deer country and has only in the past few years seen a few whitetails creeping in, mostly in the fertile agricultural valleys north of Salt Lake City. You'll find mule deer everywhere in Utah, from the classic mountain ranges of the north, northeastern and central parts of the state, to the deserts of the west, and the oak brush of the east and south.

Over 300,000 mule deer live in Utah presently, but this number can swell when the winters are mild and/or the habitat is in good shape. Most years see hunters in Utah harvesting upwards of 30,000 animals, and this, too, can fluctuate significantly as the weather dictates.

Mule Deer Seasons.

Although there are a variety of good limited-entry hunts in Utah (obtain a big game proclamation from the Division of Wildlife for all the details), there is also a general rifle season starting on the Saturday nearest October 20 and running for 9 days. Archers take to the field the weekend before Labor Day and hunt into October, while the muzzleloader season starts two days after the rifle season ends. Don't overlook the muzzleloader hunt. Sure, the bucks have been pressured. But if the rifle season started sometime after the 20th, you'll be able to hunt in November and possibly benefit from some early rutting activity. Find the does and wait there for the bucks to do the same.

Licenses and Allocation.

"In Utah, you have to choose one weapon you wish to hunt deer with – rifle, bow or muzzleloader – and that's it for the year," said Mike Welch of the Utah Division of Wildlife. For the limited-entry hunts, nonresidents are eligible for 10% of the total tags available in a unit. The state's general hunts don't have a draw, but the number of licenses available are limited so buy early as it's first-come, first-served. The south and east units sell out very quickly. The north takes a little longer, but you should still buy early or all the tags will be gone. Nonresidents pay $198 for a general deer license, residents $25.

Top Mule Deer Areas.

"The mountains in the north are where you'll generally find the densest mule deer populations," said Welch. "But the north can also be hit hard by winters, which can really cut into the herd there, so you need to know what's been happening with the weather."

Welch points out that the central and southern areas are often more popular among hunters. But even in fair to good years the north will carry more deer per square mile of habitat.

What about big bucks?

"Look to limited-entry units and private land," said Welch. "All areas of the state can and do produce bragging-sized bucks. But in general, hunting pressure is heavy in Utah, and the bucks need the protection offered by limited-entry or private land to grow to a ripe old age and carry truly big antlers."

Public and Private Land.

"Seventy-six percent of Utah is public land," said Welch, "so there are plenty of opportunities to hunt some real good mule deer country. Private land hunting is becoming big business in the state, simply because the landowners are realizing the value of big mule deer bucks. You might pay anywhere from $25 to basically get through a locked gate or thousands of dollars on one of the classic big-buck ranches."

For more information contact:

Utah Division of Wildlife Resources
1594 West North Temple - Suite 2110
P.O. Box 146301
Salt Lake City, UT 84114-6301
801-538-4700

Washington

Mule Deer Habitat, Herds and Harvest.

Most Washington mule deer inhabit a Ponderosa pine-type habitat, according to Rolf Johnson of the Department of Fish and Wildlife.

"You'll find them at the Cascade crest down through the lodgepole, but most of the muleys are in the mid-level Ponderosa pine habitats, down to their winter range of Ponderosa and grasslands," he said. "There is also some good shrub steppe (sage and grass) habitat."

About 140,000 mule deer live in Washington, and they probably account for one-third of the 35,000 deer taken annually in the state. The rest of the deer killed are blacktails and whitetails. In general, Washington has a 25% hunter success ratio, which drops for archery hunters but notches up a bit for muzzleloaders.

Mule Deer Seasons.

Archery season runs the month of September and then again from the day before Thanksgiving to December 15th. The general rifle season starts on the first Saturday in October and lasts for nine days. There are also some early high-country buck seasons. Muzzleloaders have the seven days prior to the general rifle season, plus the same dates as the late archery season. Only 10 percent of mule deer units are open to muzzleloader hunting, though.

Licenses and Allocation.

Licenses can be had over-the-counter, for both residents ($15 license plus $18 for a deer tag) and non-residents ($150 license plus $60 tag). No drawing means you can always get a license, but hunting pressure is heavy.

"With over 5.5 million residents, we're the most heavily populated Western state, and we have the smallest land area," said Johnson.

Top Mule Deer Areas.

The northcentral part of the state, particularly Okanogan County, traditionally carries the highest mule deer densities. The biggest bucks seem to be coming from the Wilson Creek Private Lands Management area, but expect to pay as much as $6,000 or more for a permit there, where the landowners sell the hunts and control the access.

Public and Private Land.

Washington has good amounts of public land, with good hunting. That is a plus. In addition, timber companies own a lot of land here and traditionally open them to hunting without a fee. To top it off, many roads are getting closed off, which is good news for limiting ATV and other vehicular access to every nook and cranny. That gives the hard-working, hard-walking hunter a fighting chance at finding a secluded canyon and some big bucks.

For more information contact:

Washington Department of Fish
   and Wildlife
600 Capitol Way N.
Olympia, WA 98501-1091
360-902-2200

Wyoming

Mule Deer Habitat, Herds and Harvest.

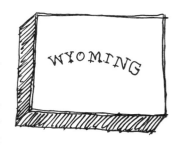

Wyoming is mule deer country, period. You can't go wrong in selecting a region to hunt. Deer can be found from the prairies of the eastern and central parts of the state, to the foothills and mountain ranges that begin to rise in those central regions, to the true mountainous areas of western and southwestern Wyoming. So how do you select a place to find one of Wyoming's 450,000 mule deer? Pick the experience you'd like. For wilderness hunts, try the mountains of central, western or northwestern Wyoming. You'll need a guide in the designated wilderness areas here. For starkly beautiful country and a chance at huge bucks, go to the southwestern part of the state. To see a lot of deer, head to the prairies. You'll be surprised at the bragging-sized bucks you can find there on the private lands where they get a chance to grow up. Hunter success is good throughout Wyoming, trending higher in the central and eastern regions.

Mule Deer Seasons.

Archery seasons run from August 15 or September 1, depending on the unit, through September. Rifle seasons generally occur in October, running two to three weeks per unit. Wyoming is another state where the hunting is closely managed by region and by unit. You'll find different season dates across the state.

Licenses and Allocation.

In Wyoming, licenses are given out through a drawing, with applications due at the end of March and the drawing taking place in July. It's excruciating to wait that long to see if you get a tag. But it's worth it when you finally get it in the mail. In some units, you do have to be lucky to get a license, as the big bucks or a lot of public land will draw the applications in like mad.

If you find a good outfitter who hunts private land or you find some access yourself, your drawing odds may improve because of the decreased competition for tags. Call Game and Fish to obtain an application and copy of regulations, as well as a "Demand Index" that outlines application numbers and success rates for each unit for the previous year.

At present, nonresident deer licenses cost $195 in Wyoming, while residents pay $22. There is a nonresident "special hunt" permit for $295. A conservation stamp is also required. It costs $5. Archery hunters must win a license in the general lottery then, in addition, must purchase a $20 archery permit. You can do that when you reach Wyoming, if you wish.

Top Mule Deer Areas.

"Wyoming has a high buck:doe ratio across the state," said Jay Lawson of the Wyoming Game and Fish Department. "So, there are good bucks throughout the state. There are some old bucks, which means big bucks, in every region."

Those words, "in every region," are important. You still have to hunt hard and hunt smart for the big ones. For big bucks, think about the Big Horns, the Tetons, the Hoback Basin and the Wyoming Range of the southwest part of the state. Campbell, Converse, Natrona and Niobrara counties are also good for big bucks and for numbers of deer, but plan your access.

Public and Private Land.

"Wyoming is half public land, but much of the access is controlled privately so be very cautious and do your homework before applying for a unit," said Lawson.

For instance, a unit may be 50 percent public land (you'll see this figure in the application booklet), but all the access may be controlled by the ranchers of the area, whose private land is intermingled in a checkerboard fashion. Bottom line: Assure public access or secure a private land hunting place at a fee you're comfortable with, or get a good outfitter, before applying for a specific region or unit. Nevertheless, many regions of the state offer extensive blocks of National Forest and BLM land you can reach, and then wander to your heart's content.

For more information contact:

Wyoming Game and Fish Department
5400 Bishop Blvd.
Cheyenne, WY 82006
307-777-4600

Chapter 12

Planning the Hunt

Introduction

If you live in the West and have traditional mule deer hunting haunts in your own or neighboring states, you're lucky. If you're not that lucky, the initial challenges of selecting a state and locale to hunt muleys, and then planning efficiently and effectively to make sure you're in a good area and have a good hunt, often seem overwhelming.

The step-by-step plan in this chapter, along with all the detailed information on where to get information, will make the planning process easy and enjoyable.

There's no better way to spend some wintry evenings than on the phone, or writing letters, or reading letters and brochures you've received, concerning mule deer hunting. All are part of the process of planning the mule deer hunt you've been dreaming of.

Come to think of it, even if you're a Westerner already, the information here will be helpful if you ever decide to, or need to, look up some new stompin' grounds.

No matter where you're coming from, planning the hunt can and should be fun.

Think of it as an essential first step that may well be the most important ingredient to your success. You want to settle on a piece of mule deer country where the hunting opportunities will be good, and where you can be comfortable, rested and well-fed to make the most of your time in the field. Mule deer country is a special place; good planning will ensure that you enjoy your time there to the fullest, and make the most of every minute you're in the field.

So get ready to do some old-fashioned visiting over the phone and some letter-writing. You'll be pleasantly surprised by all the information and Western hospitality you'll receive in return. After all, in almost all mule deer country, hunters and their dollars provide a significant boost to local economies. The "natives," from game biologists, game wardens and sporting goods store owners to meat locker people, cafe operators and shop owners, want you to come to their region, have a good time and a good hunt, leave a few dollars, and come back again.

THE HUNT PLANNING PYRAMID

Think of the process of planning your mule deer hunt as an inverted pyramid. Your challenge, and it truly is a part of the hunt, is to work your way up the pyramid, narrowing your choices and making decisions from level to level. It's really quite simple.

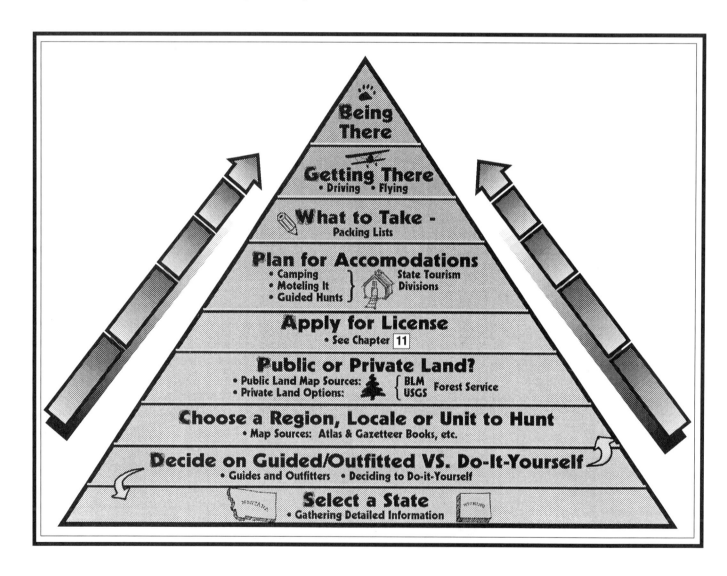

SELECT A STATE

The preceding chapter, "Mule Deer State-by-State" offers a good first step to selecting a state in which to hunt. Learning about the deer herds and trends, trophy potential, topography and available hunting opportunities will help you choose a certain state or two. So will season timing, the timing of your own personal commitments, license costs and fees and other factors unique to you.

Start by writing or calling the game agencies of the states you're interested in. These addresses and phone numbers are listed in Chapter 11. Request mule deer hunting information in detail. Ask for season dates, application deadlines, herd information and trends, "draw" statistics and harvest statistics with hunting success rates for the state's various hunting regions or units.

Even if hunting information for the upcoming season is not yet printed, ask for last year's information to get you started. Then request to be on the mailing list when new application or other information is out. Chances are seasons will be fairly similar year to year.

You should be able to get some of this information as printed material from the information officer you speak to on the phone. Always try to get at least to the information specialist level as you look for information. But it's very important to then try to get one more level into the organization. You want to speak to the game biologists and law enforcement staff that are there at headquarters. These people are incredibly knowledgeable about their state's resources and can give you excellent overviews and insights. They are also great starting points for discovering what regions might offer the best big buck potential, high success rates, good chances in the license draw, whatever aspects you're most interested in.

Don't be afraid to ask to talk to these people. You'll be surprised at how easy it is to get through, and how happy they will be to share information.

Application procedures and license drawing rules vary from state to state, and can even change from year to year within states. Write or call early to get all the details.

Application deadlines are especially important, as most states conduct draws for mule deer tags. Note these deadlines and begin the hunt planning process well in advance. A year of lead time is not too much as you choose where and when you want to hunt. Most application periods are in the late winter and spring, so you'll want to start your research as early as the fall before the one you want to hunt.

At this stage of the Hunt Planning Pyramid, you may have more than one state still in consideration. That's okay. The higher levels of the pyramid will help you narrow your focus. In the end, any state with mule deer hunting is a good one. It's the hunt you want that counts. That hunt could be in the Missouri River breaks in Montana. Or perhaps you could end up watching the irrigated hay meadows of an eastern Wyoming ranch or riding horseback high in an Idaho wilderness area. You might be probing for big bucks on the Colorado plateau or vying for a trophy in the mountains of northern New Mexico or Arizona. Maybe you'll find yourself stalking wide-racked Utah bucks in lush fir and aspen mountains high above the desert floor.

The Right Approach to Information Gathering

In my opinion, there's a right way and a wrong way to go about gathering information, no matter who you're talking to . It could be a game biologist in Wyoming, a game warden in Colorado, a taxidermist in Utah, an outfitter in Idaho, a sporting goods store owner in Montana, or anyone else in mule deer country. In any case, you've got to do it correctly.

ON THE PHONE: Remember that the other person is busy. So be courteous, friendly and to-the-point. I like to have a little script jotted down so that I don't stumble or ramble. Say who you are and what you're calling about. Have several specific questions ready and written down, and a notebook and pencil in hand to take notes as you listen.

Do not say, "I'm looking for a place to hunt mule deer and I want to know where the big bucks are, and where there are tons of them so I can take my pick."

That attitude won't get you anywhere, because all the listener hears is someone unwilling to do any homework. If you start like that, information won't flow.

A better approach is something like this. "Hello. My name is _____. I live in (state) and I'm interested in coming out mule deer hunting to (state or area) next fall. I'm looking for some information and was wondering if I could ask you just a few questions to help me locate some good areas. Would you have just a couple minutes to talk?" Then, have suitable questions ready for the particular expert you're talking to.

Guaranteed, you'll get at least a couple minutes of their time, or a time when you could call back if the timing of this particular call isn't perfect.

IN A LETTER: The same rule applies. You're gathering information, not looking for a place to hunt. Say so in your introduction, and briefly list exactly the information you want. Reading time is short for busy people with a pile of mail. Chances are you may not get an extensive personalized letter back but you'd be surprised at the harvest reports, draw statistics, herd trends and other information that is available for the asking.

Of course, outfitters will send you their brochures, and these are a good start to planning that type of hunt. If your interest is high, by all means call back and visit awhile.

CALL OR WRITE?: My general rule of thumb is this: A phone call will always net you more information. You may glean the names of other contacts in the state or region in the course of a conversation, and you'll get any mailed information back sooner. Letters are okay if the nature of your request is for reports or other printed information. But lean towards the phone. A call costs more than a stamp, but you'll discover what you're needing to know more efficiently.

TJC

DECIDE ON A GUIDE OR GO IT ALONE

This is an important decision, and a very personal one.

On the one hand, a guided hunt is expensive. You'll have to do your homework (we'll suggest how) to assure you're getting involved with a reputable outfit. But if you go this route, much of the other work will be done for you. That includes things like locating an area to hunt (be it public or private land), accommodations and food. If the outfitter is good he or she will tell you exactly what you need to bring. That will take those nagging worries away, and all you have to do is get there.

A middle ground exists in the guided hunt/do-it-yourself continuum, and that's working with an outfitter who will drop you at a sup-plied camp in good mule deer country. This is a different proposition altogether. You'll be largely on your own, with equipment others provide, in country you may not know. Do your homework on exactly where you'll be hunting and who you'll be dealing with, and you should be in good shape.

Finally, you can do the hunt on your own. This is always the lowest cost route because you're not paying someone else to provide services like feeding you, getting you to the hunting grounds, probably hunting right beside you every step of the way, and packing your meat and trophy out. This route is also the most work on your part, but it can also be very affordable and rewarding.

A Wyoming hunting camp.

Guides and Outfitters

If you choose to take this trail, the first step to selecting a reputable guide or outfitter is to obtain a list of licensed guides from the organization that licenses or regulates that line of business in the state you wish to hunt. Here's a list:

Arizona:

The Game and Fish Department licenses guides. See Chapter 11 for address and phone number

California:

The Department of Fish and Game licenses guides. See Chapter 11 for address and phone number. Contact the License and Revenue Branch.

Colorado:

Department of Regulatory Agents
1560 Broadway, Suite 1340
Denver, Colorado 80202
303-894-7778

Kansas:

The Department of Wildlife and Parks certifies hunting and fishing guides, and maintains a listing. See Chapter 11 for address and phone.

Idaho:

Outfitters & Guides Licensing Board
1365 N. Orchard Room 172
Boise, ID 83706
208-327-7380

Montana:

Board of Outfitters
Arcade Building - Lower Level
111 N. Jackson - P.O. Box 200513
Helena, MT 59620-0513

Nebraska:

Does not have this type of organization.

Nevada:

The Division of Wildlife's Law Enforcement area licenses outfitters and guides. See Chapter 11 for address and phone number.

New Mexico:

The Department of Game and Fish licenses outfitters and guides. See Chapter 11 for address and phone number.

North Dakota:

Contact the Game and Fish Department's Licensing Bureau. See Chapter 11 for address and phone number.

Oklahoma:

Does not have this type of organization.

Oregon:

State Marine Board
P.O. Box 14145
Salem, OR 97309
503-378-8587

South Dakota:

Professional Guides and
  Outfitters Association
P.O. Box 703
Pierre, S.D. 57501
Although this association is not regulated by the state, it still records the state's outfitters and guides.

Texas:

Does not have this type of organization.

Utah:

Does not register guides or outfitters.

Washington:

Outfitters & Guides Association
22845 NE 8 - Suite 331
Redmond, WA 98053
Although this association is not regulated by the state, it still records the state's outfitters and guides

Wyoming:

State Board of Outfitters and
  Professional Guides
1750 Westland Road, Suite 166
Cheyenne, WY 82002
307-777-5323

These above organizations can serve as basic resources for locating guides and outfitters in each state. But an even more important use for the lists you receive may be to make sure that outfits you learn about from other sources are in fact registered, licensed, reputable and on the list. This is important for your comfort level, and also because in some states, like Wyoming, it is illegal to contract an outfitter or guide who is not licensed by the state.

The very best way to quickly find good guides and outfitters is by word-of-mouth from someone who had a good hunt. Another is magazine ads, keeping in mind the previous paragraph's advice. A third is sportsman's shows. Another good source that many people overlook are chambers of commerce in specific towns within regions you're interested in. Just call information to get the number of the chamber, and ask a few questions. Chances are, they have a list of local guides and outfitters available.

Write or call outfits you hear about or that sound good to get some more information. Calling may be your best bet because it gives you a chance to talk with someone and at least get a feel for what they're like.

Guides and Outfitters: Cardinal Rules

Here is Cardinal Rule Number One when selecting a guide or outfitter: GET REFERENCES.

Past performance is almost always the best indicator of the quality of services on future hunts. Talking to someone you know is best. Any reputable outfitter will give you a list of past customers to talk to. Although you probably won't find any truly unsatisfied ones on the list provided, probe the ones you do visit with. Be friendly. Get them talking by asking about their hunt and listening to their tales. Everyone loves to tell their hunting stories. Then ask for some honest feedback on their hunt. Cardinal rule number two (below) will give

you additional ideas on what types of questions to ask when obtaining this reference.

Here is Cardinal Rule Number Two on selecting a guide or outfitter: UNDERSTAND TOTALLY WHAT IS PROVIDED, AND WHAT IS YOUR RESPONSIBILITY.

What is the total cost? Where will you eat? Who cooks? Where will you sleep? Will you get picked up at an airport, met somewhere, or drive right to camp? What equipment should you bring? Be sure to ask about weather possibilities. What's the terrain like where you will be hunting? Will you be hunting private land? Will you hunt public land? Public land hunts can be superb but remember that competition from other hunters or camps often can't be controlled, like it can on private land. What about meat and trophy care? Who will do it, where, and at what cost? How many guides per hunter? How many hunters in camp? What's the hunting style? Does it fit your style, desires and capabilities?

Expect to pay anywhere from $2,500 to $5,000 for a four- or five-day, guided mule deer hunt (1998 dollars). Of course the cost varies with locale, trophy buck potential and length of hunt. Of course, $5,000 is by no means the limit. There's a lot of sky out there in that respect! But you'll truly be getting the hunt of a lifetime.

If you go with a complete hunt package, much of the rest of the work associated with the Hunt Planning Pyramid is done for you.

Deciding to Do It Yourself

For most hunters, though, a fully guided and outfitted hunt is a real luxury. We might only have the opportunity and funds to do it a time or two in a hunting career. That makes selecting the right outfitter and hunt a very important process. But there's no reason to stay home when the family budget is tight.

For a fraction of the cost of a guided hunt, you can have a great hunt on your own and, yes, bag a good buck. Many of us decide to go it alone, especially if we like to do things affordably. If you live in the West already, it's even easier to do it right and have a spectacular time. Here's how, as we work our way up the Hunt Planning Pyramid.

CHOOSE A REGION, LOCALE OR UNIT TO HUNT

Every Western state is big, and each offers a variety of mule deer country. So how do you begin to focus on specific regions, areas or units to hunt? The best way is to study the harvest statistics and trends and other information you have received from the state, and then start making some more phone calls.

The best thing to do now is to start contacting fish and game department personnel. Only this time, you're not going to be talking to the experts in Denver, Cheyenne, Helena, Boise, Salt Lake City, Santa Fe or any other capital-city headquarters locations. You must branch out and talk to experts of a different kind, those in the field.

From the information you received while selecting the state, determine which branch offices reside in or near the areas you've learned about, then call. Use a script similar to the one outlined previously. Ask to talk to the local game warden, or assistant game warden, or a game biologist or wildlife researcher. Talk to anyone with hands-on duties in the field, or at least someone who has contact with those who are out in the field regularly.

This is where you will really begin zeroing in on a place to hunt. Ask about herd trends in the area. Ask about recent winters and public land options. Discuss, the private land situation and options. Ask if a good percentage of bucks make it through the hunting seasons to be bigger next year. This question gives you information on trophy potential without saying it outright. Ask about the terrain. You'll find that if you start asking a few questions in a polite manner, most of the information will flow freely.

An Example

Here's a purely hypothetical example of how this process should be working, at this point.

Through calls to the Colorado, Montana and Wyoming fish and game headquarters, and information you've received via mail, you've determined Wyoming is the state for you because: the license price fits your budget; there are plenty of draw units which should keep hunting pressure under control; recent mild winters; a good article on Wyoming mule deer hunting in a recent magazine; and lots of hunt units open in early October so you can be home for your daughter's birthday on the 25th.

A biologist at headquarters said that the central part of the state has had some exceptionally mild winters and herds are healthy. He added that herds in the far west seem to be coming back from a drought a couple years ago, but hunters aren't streaming in yet. So, you place calls to regional offices in Casper and Rock Springs, and reach a research biologist in one office and, after five tries, you finally catch a game warden in the other office.

Both conversations were good ones, but that western Wyoming idea is really intriguing you. The game warden said, barring a bad blizzard yet this winter, there should be a nice crop of 2 1/2 to 3 1/2 year-old bucks. The draw percentages have been decent in the area and you heard about several National Forests and some chunks of BLM land where you can get off the beaten path with a little work. Now you may even have a hunt unit number in hand.

Map Sources for Choosing a Region, Locale or Unit

There are several basic maps you'll want to have in hand at this stage of planning your hunt. One is a state highway map, available from the state's tourism department. Another is the wildlife division's map of hunting units.

But at this stage, one of the best maps you can have is an "Atlas & Gazetteer" for the state you're investigating. These large books have more than 100 pages of quadrangular maps covering the entire state. There is a surprising amount of detail on these maps. There's more than enough to get your search for a hunting place started, and certainly enough to locate general areas that people will be talking to you about.

During the course of planning your hunt, you will want to use additional maps as well, because at a scale of 1:150,000, the Atlas & Gazetteer maps won't help you accurately identify every specific property boundary and land feature. The 1:150,000 scale means that one unit of measure on the map equals 150,000 units of the same unit of measure on the ground. For exam-

ple, 1 inch on the map would equal 150,000 inches on the ground which is 12,500 feet or 2.37 miles. Still, these maps are excellent tools to begin your search. They indicate public and private land boundaries in a general way, and you'll be able to locate roads from blacktop highways all the way down to some two-track trails. These map books also offer good information to get you started on finding accommodations, campgrounds and other information of interest.

Currently all the Western states except New Mexico are covered. Expect to pay up to $19.95, but it's a good value. You can find Atlas & Gazetteers in bookstores, sporting goods stores and some catalogs.

Or write or call:

DeLorme Mapping Company
Two DeLorme Drive, P.O. Box 298
Yarmouth, ME 04096
800-452-5931 or 207-865-4171

PUBLIC OR PRIVATE LAND?

Vast Public Land Resources

The majority of the West is publicly owned. Between national forests and other Forest Service lands, Bureau of Land Management (BLM) lands, state forests, other state acreage and national grasslands, you have millions of acres you can hunt free of charge — just because, as a U.S. citizen, you own the land. And if you're coming from Canada or another country, you have the right to use this land as well.

But free access can also mean high use. Unless you plan your hunt well, and this means devising an action plan to get away from the roads to do your hunting, don't expect to find mature bucks. This is not to discourage you. It is a fact that annually many of the biggest mule deer

bucks taken come from public land. But these deer are not shot roadside or along some trail. They're in the hinterlands, far off the beaten path. Remember, few hunters ever venture more than a half-mile off any road or trail. Finding your own secret hunting spot is not rocket science. All it takes is a little preliminary map work, and then some gumption and footwork.

Great Private Land Opportunities

That said about public land, private land is a definite and good option. The advantages of a private land hunt are substantial. Two of the biggest advantages include: controlled access, which should equate to less competition from other hunters; and high-quality animals to hunt.

Associated with private-land hunting is what's usually called a "trespass fee." It may go by another name depending on the state and region. This fee usually covers the entire bow or rifle deer season, and is your payment to the landowner in return for access on their land. Occasionally such a fee is paid on a per-day basis.

The trespass fee is a reality in the modern West, and the system works. Costs vary according to the region and how much acreage you're getting access to, but may range anywhere from $100 to $1,000 or more for a season. The norm seems to run around $200 to $250.

The cost is usually well worth it. There's nothing like heading off to a chunk of good country and knowing you're going to be the only one hunting there. You'll usually get a place to park your camper or tent in the deal.

The Final Decision

So which way do you go, public or private land? Chances are, when you were selecting a region or unit at the previous level of the Hunt Planning Pyramid, you got steered one way or the other. If both are still options, make some calls and get more information to make your choice. Here's how.

Public Land: Map Sources and More

BLM MAPS. The absolute best maps for locating public land and determining access to it are Bureau of Land Management 1:100,000 scale topographic maps, also known as surface management maps.

These maps are detailed right down to specific, clear color keys that show land ownership not only of BLM land but also national forests, state forests and others. You can locate a specific area to hunt on a map like this, make a plan for getting away from roads and two-

BLM surface management maps. The different shades on the background map represent various land ownership status.

tracks (unless new ones were forged since creation of the map), and get an excellent idea of the lay of the land and topographical features such as foothills, mountains, canyons, coulees, hillsides, flats, streams, springs and so forth. At the 1:100,000 scale, 1 inch on the map equals about 1.58 miles on the ground.

The best way to get these maps is to call or write the BLM office in that state (a list follows). You'll want to start by obtaining an index to figure out which maps to order. In some cases, the BLM personnel may be able to help you figure out which maps to get right over the phone, if you know the county and/or hunting units you're interested in. These maps will probably cost between $4 and $5 each.

It may be a good idea to call ahead and check with local land management agencies to make sure there haven't been recent land sales and exchanges that have changed the ownership status of lands. Most of these sales are being accomplished to "block up" larger tracts of public lands for the public to use, and you'll want to find out where these new and larger tracts are.

Here are addresses and phone numbers for state or regional offices of the BLM:

Arizona Sate Office - Bureau of
    Land Management
222 North Central Ave.
Phoenix, AZ 85004-2208
602-417-9200

California State Office - Bureau of
    Land Management
2135 Butano Drive
Sacramento, CA 95825-0451
916-978-4400

Colorado State Office - Bureau of
    Land Management
2850 Youngfield Street
Lakewood, CO 80125
303-239-3600

Idaho State Office -- Bureau of
    Land Management
1387 S. Vennell Way
Boise, ID 83709
208-373-4000

Montana State Office -- Bureau of
    Land Management
    (Includes North and South Dakota)
222 North 32nd Street
P.O. Box 36800
Billings, MT 59107
406-255-2885

Nevada State Office - Bureau of
    Land Management
1340 Financial Blvd.
P.O. Box 12000
Reno, NV 89520-0006
702-785-6500

New Mexico State Office - Bureau of
    Land Management
(Includes Oklahoma, Texas and Kansas)
1474 Rodeo Road - P.O. Box 27115
Santa Fe, NM 87502-0115
505-438-7400

Oregon/Washington State Office - Bureau of
    Land Management
1515 SW 5th - P.O. Box 2965
Portland, OR 97208-2965
503-952-6001

Utah State Office - Bureau of
    Land Management
324 South State Street - Suite 400
P.O. Box 45155
Salt Lake City, UT 84145-0155
801-539-4001

Wyoming State Office - Bureau of
    Land Management (includes Nebraska)
5353 Yellowstone Road - P.O. Box 1828
Cheyenne WY 82003-1828
307-775-6256

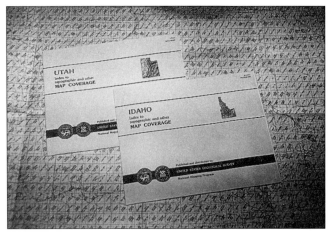

When you write or call the USGS, you'll receive indexes like these. They list all the 1:24,000 scale maps — and there are a lot of them — available for each state. Plus, a variety of other good maps will be listed.

USGS MAPS. Topographic maps from the United States Geological Survey (USGS) provide even more detail than BLM maps. These are the resources for getting into the nitty-gritty such as finding secluded canyons or spots that are truly far from any road. At a scale of 1:24,000, you can see how the detail has increased from where we started; one inch on this type of map would equate to just about 670 yards. Put another way, it takes about 2-1/2" on the map to cover a mile on the ground. Now that's some detail!

It's fairly tricky business getting the right maps so ask detailed questions when you call or write, and be sure to call for help if you even think you might need it when you're ordering maps. There are very friendly and efficient people in this office. Note that before ordering you'll need to receive a catalog and index of the state or states you're interested in. This will help you select the specific maps you need.

One of "Murphy's Laws of Maps" you'll discover here is that the spot you really want to hunt lies at the convergence of four of these

maps! Actually, it's a function of the detail you're getting into. So plan to shell out for more than one map

The source for USGS topographic maps:

United States Geological Survey
Branch of Information Services
Box 25286
Building 810 Denver Federal Center
Denver, CO 80225
303-202-4700

FOREST SERVICE MAPS. National forests are second in acreage only to BLM land in western public lands. Call or write one of the six regional offices listed below for maps and information on specific forests in those regions. Address your letters to the U.S. Forest Service at:

Region 1

Montana, Northern Idaho, North Dakota, Northwestern South Dakota
Federal Building, P.O. Box 7669
Missoula, MT 59807
406-329-3511

Region 2

Colorado, Eastern Wyoming, Kansas, Nebraska, Southwestern South Dakota
740 Simms
P.O. Box 25127
Lakewood, CO 80225
303-275-5350

Region 3

Arizona, New Mexico
Federal Building
517 Gold Ave. S.W.
Albuquerque, NM 87102
505-842-3292

Region 4

Nevada, Utah, Southern Idaho, Western Wyoming
Federal Building
324 25th St.
Ogden, UT 84401
801-625-5306

Region 5

California
630 Sansome St.
San Francisco, CA 94111
415-705-2869

Region 6

Oregon, Washington
Nature of the Northwest
800 N.E. Oregon St.
Room 177
Portland, OR 97232
503-872-2750

STATE FOREST MAPS. Contact that state's fish and game agency (see Chapter 11 for a listing and phone numbers) to obtain information and maps on forest lands under that state's jurisdiction.

From your conversations with people on the local or regional level, as well as these map sources, you'll find good access to thousands upon thousand of acres of publicly owned land to hunt. Use your phone, pen or PC to correspond with the types of people discussed, and the map resources listed, and you'll get all the information you'll need.

One final note about public lands in the West. Be sure to inquire about state and local laws and customs regarding trespass, even if you plan on hunting only on public land. In many places there is a real mix of public and private land. It is important to know what your limitations are, as far as crossing private land to reach public land. Generally it is not allowed without permission from the landowner or lessee. And every state has different laws regarding the marking of private land. In Utah, for instance, if you see every third fence post with its top painted blaze orange, private land lays behind the barbed wire.

Private Land Options

Used to be that in many areas of the West the price of hunting on private land was a cup of coffee at the kitchen table and a handshake. The times have changed. That doesn't mean that you can't hunt private land. You can. And you can do it without a guide or outfitter, and there are still good values for your dollar. In fact, in most all the Western states, landowners from big corporate outfits to family-owned and operated homesteads charge what we've called the "trespass fee."

Actually, it's a good deal. For a daily or season fee, you'll get access. Competition from other hunters is reduced. The quality of the animals and hunting is often very high, and the landowner is getting a fair return for some use of the land that he or she has worked so hard to buy, maintain and make a living from.

How do you find these spots?

The best and easiest way is, as usual, word of mouth from friends and acquaintances who may have gone west and hunted like this. Make some calls in your own area to hunters you know of that hunt in the West annually.

Another good way is to get on the phone, call information for the area code of the region you're focusing on, and ask for the chambers of commerce in towns close to where you want to hunt. There are also county tourism offices. Call these organizations and ask if they have lists of local ranches or landowners who allow, or might allow, hunting for a fee.

Now these two methods are perfectly good ones for finding some prime private land to hunt. But they are also relatively easy, which means the land may well be booked full for hunting. So here are some other ideas for ferreting out private land places to hunt on your own.

Ads. Take out an ad in the local paper for the area you're focusing on. Gear it to be friendly and positive, saying that you're looking for private land to hunt deer on, and are willing to pay a fee. Provide a number for collect calls for responses, or an address to write.

One person we know achieved excellent results. He got several responses and ultimately secured 20,000 acres to hunt by placing an ad that started "Father and sons looking for deer hunting lands to lease for next hunting season." The keys are honesty and conveying that you are respectable and trustworthy. Place the ad where ranchers and landowners might be reading, such as livestock or farm/ranch equipment classifieds, the vehicle classifieds, or the real estate section; ask the newspaper for advice here.

County plat maps. Call the county seat for the area you're targeting, and obtain a copy of the county plat map showing land ownership. This is public information that should be available to you. Try to locate some target landowners with substantial acreage, then send extremely polite and personalized letters asking about hunting. Tell them you want to hunt mule deer in the area, need a spot to hunt, are responsible, and willing to pay a trespass fee.

This is very important: Include a stamped, self-addressed envelope so replying is easy for the rancher or landowner. If you wish, offer your phone number for a collect call. If you get a "sorry, but we can't help you" letter back, don't be surprised if you get the name and address of someone else you might try. As a common courtesy, don't call these landowners until you've received a positive response. Like you, they are busy and don't need extra phone calls.

Local stores. One other method is to call local sporting goods stores in the area you're planning to hunt, and put the question to them. They may know of local ranchers, land-

owners or other resources. You can get the sporting goods store addresses and phone numbers by writing the local chamber of commerce for information on the area; you'll get plenty of brochures on the town and/or county, with advertisements for its businesses.

Courtesy is key. No matter what method you use, courtesy and a good attitude will get you everywhere. Even though you'll be paying a fee, the rancher's land, fences, gates, equipment and livestock are worth more towards his or her livelihood than your trespass fee. You need to portray your trustworthiness.

When zeroing in on a place to hunt, be sure to ask questions about how many other hunters are being allowed on the acreage, and the quality of bucks that might be available; this should help you make some decisions. And don't forget that once you set up a rapport, you can use the rancher or landowner sparingly – mostly once you're out there and getting ready to hunt – as a resource to point you in the right directions for hunting the kind of bucks you're interested in.

Be prepared to sign a release. This is standard procedure. It releases the landowner from any responsibility should you have an accident of any type on ranch lands.

Much of the West is public, it's true. But there's a lot of West out there. That means private lands are substantial as well. These lands harbor some superb mule deer hunting. With a little work you can get access to a chunk of this prime land, at a decent value for your dollar even in this day and age.

APPLY FOR LICENSES AND TAGS

Apply for licenses and tags once you've identified where you'll be hunting. If you're heading for public land, you may not yet know the exact drainage or mountain or chunk of prairie you'll be hunting, but knowing you have access is good enough for now. If you're hunting private land, you should be very sure of exactly where you're hunting; the last thing you want to do is apply for and get a tag, then not have access to hunting land.

Follow the state's instructions and deadlines to a "T" when you apply. With hundreds or thousands of applications coming in per hunt unit, yours will be kicked out if it's not done properly and on time. The department may or may not have time to call you back to clarify questions.

One good tip here is to run your application past a hunting buddy before you send it in. Do this to be sure you've completed everything, done it correctly, and signed where needed. It's worth the effort.

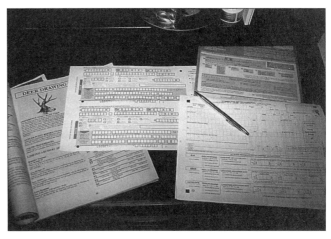

Applying for the license draws can be fairly involved. It's a good idea to have a buddy review your completed application before sending it in, just to be sure you filled out and signed everything you needed to.

PLAN FOR ACCOMMODATIONS

Looking back to the hypothetical example we started before, let's say you've located big chunks of both BLM lands and national forest ground to hunt in that western Wyoming unit. Now, where do you stay? Do you camp right out in mule deer country? Pull a trailer or motorhome into a maintained campground? Or stay in town at a motel and drive out to a hunting area each day?

Camping

National forest campgrounds are often good places for pulling in your camper or a motorhome. You can even set up a tent. But these are often busy places during deer season, especially around opening day. The advantages include a few more creature comforts than you might get with the next idea.

That idea is that visitors to the West are often surprised that you can camp most anywhere on BLM or national forest lands. That can make for a very good hunt because you can get closer to mule deer hunting country. You'll spend less time in transit to your hunting area, and probably be able to get out earlier and stay later, which equals more quality hunting time. And you can get away from the beaten path with less effort each day. That's what you want anyway if you're serious about finding some big mule deer.

While it's true that hunting pressure is often fairly well controlled in the West through lottery draws and other permit systems for licenses, there's still nothing like getting totally away from everyone else and hunting muleys one-on-one.

Call the Bureau of Land Management and national forest offices listed previously to obtain details on campgrounds, and rules for camping on those lands. Talk to local chambers of commerce, county tourism organizations and state game and fish departments to get details on private and county campground opportunities, and on state facilities and rules.

Moteling It

Of course, there's nothing like a hot shower, a decent bed and a few restaurant meals. If you like these things stay at a motel in town. After all, it is a vacation and you should enjoy yourself. But what you gain in comfort in a motel you may lose through long drives in the dark to and from your hunting grounds. On the other hand, if an area doesn't work out one day, you can drive to another spot the next day without pulling camp. You're fairly flexible from a motel.

State tourism divisions, like local and county chambers of commerce, are excellent resources for accommodations within all these categories.

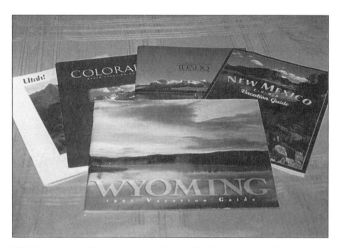

Write or call state tourism divisions for basic information on accommodations in that state.

Here is a listing of those state tourism organizations. If you're on the internet, try http:/// www.towd.com for a tourism directory with hot links to many of these organizations' web sites.

Arizona Office of Tourism
2702 North Third Street, Suite 4015
Phoenix, AZ 85009
800-842-8257

California Division of Tourism
Sacramento, CA 95812
800-GO-CALIF

Colorado Tourism Board
1624 Broadway, Suite 1700
Denver CO 80202
800-265-6723 or 800-433-2656

Kansas Travel and Tourism Division
700 S.W. Harrison Street, Suite 31300
Topeka, KS 66603-3712
800-2KANSAS

Idaho Travel Council
700 West State Street
Boise, ID 83720-2700
800-635-7820

Montana - Travel Montana
P.O. Box 7549
Missoula, MT 59807
800-847-4868 or 800-548-3390 or 800-541-1447

Nebraska Travel & Tourism Bureau
P.O. Box 94666
Lincoln, NE 68509-4666
800-228-4307

Nevada Commission on Tourism
Capitol Complex
Carson City, NV 89701
800-NEVADA-8

New Mexico Tourism
491 Old Santa Fe Trail
Santa Fe, NM 87503
800-SEE-NEWMEX or 800-733-6396

North Dakota Tourism Department
Liberty Memorial Building
604 East Boulevard
Bismarck, ND 58505
800-435-5663

Oklahoma Tourism and
    Recreation Department
15 North Robinson, Room 801
P.O. Box 52002
Oklahoma City, OK 73152-2002
800-652-OKLA

Oregon Tourism Division
775 Summer Street NE
Salem, OR 97310
800-547-7842

South Dakota Department of Tourism
711 East Wells Ave.
Pierre, SD 57501-3369
800-732-5682

Texas Tourism Division
P.O. Box 12728
Austin, TX 78711
800-8888-TEX

Utah Travel Council
Council Hall / Capitol Hill
Salt Lake City, UT 84114
800-200-1160

Washington State Tourism and
    Development Division
P.O. Box 42500
Olympia, WA 98504-2500
800-544-1800

Wyoming Division of Tourism
Interstate 25 at College Drive
Cheyenne, WY 82002
800-CALL-WYO

Guided Hunts

Of course, if you're taking a guided hunt, accommodations of some sort should be part of the deal. Be sure to define exactly what the accommodation will be. Common options include a motel in town, a ranch house or bunkhouse, or a base camp in the foothills or right up on a mountain somewhere. If possible, choose an outfitter that uses an option other than a motel in town. Sleeping in town takes away a little bit of the true flavor of the West and mule deer country.

The Case For Camping Out

As the old Dodge pickup neared the low range of bald, round-faced mountains rising out of the southern Idaho desert, I glanced sidelong at Daren Cornforth and my brother Chuck. "That's where we're opening the mule deer season tomorrow?" I wondered, almost out loud.

But as we crossed the last ranch gate and entered the BLM-owned foothills, which were just small versions of the big mound-shaped hills behind, a whole new world opened up.

The tawny color I had seen back on the flats was beautiful, waist-high grass. A mule deer doe bounced across the dirt two-track. A covey of Hungarian Partridge raced ahead of the truck and ducked into a draw. My brother's shotgunning skills – after I had scattered the covey and missed several shots – netted us three of the lovely birds for dinner.

We climbed into the higher hills. Long, narrow draws filled with quakies snaked down from the gentle ridges. From the flats below you couldn't see these trees, hidden in the moist folds of the hills' dry shoulders. We set up camp quickly and quietly in a saddle of the top ridge line, then grilled the partridge over sage coals as the orange sun sank and the October dusk started giving way to cool night. The day had been beautiful, but unusually warm.

We glassed mule deer from camp, but it was too dark to see any antlers by the time the deer came out, so we went to bed. The quiet on this bare mountain was overwhelming. Other than

Daren Cornforth and a couple of pre-hunt Hungarian partridge.

the stars, only a few lonely ranch lights twinkled, miles away on the distant flats.

We woke a half hour before dawn, and worked up one of the quakey-bottomed draws at first light. A few does and small bucks, not really alarmed and reluctant to leave, bounded out ahead of us. By mid-afternoon, the temperature was in the high 80s and we had hunted a big circle back to camp, passing shots on several smallish bucks. Sipping sodas in the shadow of our small tent, the only shade on the sage-covered ridge, we wondered where the mature bucks had gone, or if they were even here.

The only other hunter we were to see that day walked up to our camp. "Nice buck passed over this saddle two hours ago," he reported during our chat, and then was on his way. He looked as scorched and drained as we did as he headed back toward his camper rig several miles away at the base of the range.

But as the sun started sinking on another day, some life came back to us. We decided to hunt on our own for the evening. Each of us seemed to need and want some time on our own, hunting solo, in this lonely land.

My brother, knowing we had glassed a couple big deer from camp the night before, and having heard the report of the buck that had passed within spitting distance of our tent, dropped down into the steep draw behind camp. Such is his style. He just works hard in territory he has some faith in. When I heard two shots from that direction I knew he had found what he was looking for.

At last light Chuck had jumped the four-pointer out of the quakies. It was a moist, shady and cool place for a fat mule deer to spend the warm afternoon. Chuck dropped the buck as it trotted up toward the ridge, through the tall sage. He dressed the deer, then climbed back up the steep slope towards camp in the dark. Daren and I were just beginning to worry about him when the brush cracked and he strode into the light of our campfire, sleeves rolled up and a big smile on his face.

The only problem now was that the warm days were not going to let up. The buck would be fine tonight, but with another warm day in store, we would need to get him skinned and in a cooler or, at the least, into a shady camp we might find somewhere farther down the mountain.

The plan was simple. I would get the chance to hunt down the mountain in the morning as Daren and Chuck pulled camp and drove around to the base of the hills. We would meet up, then go get the buck and drag him down together.

A small breeze lapped gently at the tent as I stared out the tent flap at the crescent moon, before dawn even thought about breaking. Sleep was done, hunting was on my mind. I dressed in the bag, Daren made me hot chocolate and oatmeal by lamplight, and I was on my way by the light of the stars and the waning moon.

A half hour later I sat on a flat rock behind a sage bush and waited for shooting light. All the while I was watching the green chaparral two hundred yards across the draw. It was good, moist deer browse in this dry country. A couple twigs cracked and I got ready. I scanned the opposite hillside but saw nothing.

Then antlers came bobbing through the sage. They were heading right toward me on the slope I was sitting on. I had been looking too far! The buck closed the distance as quickly as the dawn light built. I was watching him in my scope now. At 30 yards he stopped, quartering toward me. The scope's crosshairs rested on his near shoulder. At the shot he dropped from sight.

I watched for several minutes, then picked my way carefully down the slope. I found him just as the orange sun cleared the high Bear River and Wasatch fronts far to the east. He wasn't huge, a yearling two-point, but he was beautiful in the orange light raking across the

sage, and I had got him one-on-one. I was very happy.

A couple hours later I met the old Dodge pick-up a couple miles below. Dragging the buck downslope had been a breeze. The truck's occupants were pleased to see a deer there already, then even more pleased to see it was a new buck, and that we still had last night's bigger buck up the mountain a ways.

Some days everything just works out perfectly. I took the shotgun on our walk up the quaky draw, and we traded off on shots at ruffed grouse that had pioneered the moist, brushy

Camping is a great way to really get a feel for mule deer country, enhance your overall outdoor experience and maximize your hunting time. Here's Tom and brother Chuck with a couple southern Idaho bucks.

timber lines. We even brought a couple gray-tailed birds back down with the other buck.

Now this is a good hunting story, to be sure. But its other motive is to illustrate the benefits of camping out. Being "out there" in an obscure, simple but comfortable camp made all the difference in the world. We glassed deer right from camp; enjoyed beautiful starlit nights; got to sleep a little longer, and were more rested in the mornings. Because the hunting grounds were right there, we hunted right up through the productive, witching hour of dusk and minimized back-and-forth travel time. We got to relax by a campfire; and slept right out there on the high-desert ground that our bucks had been born and raised on. We were actually living in mule deer country for a few wonderful days.

There's plenty of time for creature comforts the rest of the year. Get yourself the basic comforts out there in an obscure, secluded campsite where you won't bust the deer out of the country and then hunt hard.

TJC

WHAT TO TAKE— PACKING LIST

We all go through it before a hunting trip, asking ourselves as we feverishly pack: What do I take? Do I really need this? What about that? How many of these do I need? And so forth.

Basically there are two packing strategy extremes.

One strategy is "Take it all" or its more realistic corollary, "Take all you can." This is an okay strategy because you won't want for anything, but the sheer volume of stuff you have to keep track of is sure to weigh you down, and weigh on your mind.

The other extreme is "If in doubt, leave it out." The trick here is to be effective in cutting your load, but making the cuts judiciously so you're not left without some essential gear.

Now, every packing situation is different. Weather will be different. Terrain varies. Some hunts are guided. You might decide to stay in town or you'll be camping on your own. There's really no way to provide a single cut-and-dried packing list for a mule deer hunt. But what we can do is provide you with the following, fairly exhaustive lists. Glean what you need from each category. The idea here is to ease your mind a bit and present many of the possibilities of what you might need. Use your own packing strategy and style, along with knowledge of the hunt you're planning, to create your own list.

Weapons-Related
Rifle
Ammunition
Scope cover
Gun case
Scabbard
Sling
Gun cleaning kit
Small tool kit for emergencies
Bow
Arrows
Broadheads
Archery Gear Box (With all necessary
    accessories or tools)
Practice target
Muzzleloader
Possibles kit
Spare ramrod
Cleaning gear

Headwear
Light cap for warm days (blaze or camo)
Stocking cap or warm cap with earflaps
    and brim
Scarf
Face mask (for bowhunting)

Hands
Light gloves

Heavy gloves or mittens
Hand warmers (probably the one-use kind)

Feet

Boots (comfortable ones, light for walking and quiet for stalking)
Waterproof rubber boots and / or boots for snow / cold conditions
Extra socks (for foot-refreshing mid-day changes)
Spare set of laces

Clothes: Outerwear

Jacket (Camo, blaze or other)
Orange vest (for wear when a jacket is too warm)
Pants (wool or other soft, quiet material)
Camouflage outerwear (for archery hunting)

Clothes: Middle Layers

Sweatshirt
Wool shirt (preferred) or flannel
"Warm-up" type fleece pullover

Clothes: Inner Layer

T-shirts or polypropylene undershirts (to wick moisture)
Underwear
Turtleneck
Long underwear pants and shirts (polypropylene will wick moisture)
Cotton socks
Warm socks (woolies plus polypropylene liners for cold weather)

Day Pack

A daypack is a must for almost all Western hunting. It will hold rain gear, extra layers of clothes (for putting on or taking off as the temperature and your activity fluctuates), food and water (you must drink regularly in the dry air of the West), camera, compass and maps, and other selections on the list below. If you're hunting good country, you'll be far from camp or your vehicle. You need to be comfortable, and stay out all day. Get a quiet pack, the fleece models are good. Make sure your pack has plenty of room and pockets. When full, it will even serve as a makeshift rifle rest on top of a rock or over a sage bush. Don't worry about mashing your sandwiches; it's a small price to pay for the nice, solid shooting rest.

Day pack contents should include:

Rain gear (rolled up compactly)
Space blanket (for emergencies)
Fire kit (2 each, candles and lighters, plus tinder, in a waterproof bag)
Flashlight (check bulb, bring extra batteries taped together)
Compass
Map
License / tag
Knife
String for field-dressing
Field-dressing gloves (optional)
Small first-aid kit
Wineskin / water bottle
Rope
Deer drag harness
A few rounds of extra ammo
Save some room in the pack for food and clothing you might remove.

Meat Care

See Chapter 10 for a list of needed items. You'll also want to bring cooler(s) for cooled meat, or carrying frozen meat home

Camping Equipment

The following is a general list you'll want to adjust as needed according to your camping style. Backpacking, driving to your site, pulling an RV or camper or sleeping under the shell of your truck will all require different gear. Expand or contract the list as needed.

Tent
Rain fly
Tarps
Extra rope and spikes
Cook stove
Matches
Fuel for stove
Lantern
Fuel/batteries for lantern
Mess kit
Pots, pans, cooking utensils, eating utensils,

plates, cups
Menu plan and food (try and do some of your
    shopping in mule deer country)
Water containers
Air mattresses or sleeping pads
Sleeping bags
Alarm
Pillows
Personal stuff (soap, toothbrush and paste, etc.)
A copy of *Mule Deer: Hunting Today's Trophies*

GETTING THERE

Many hunters drive to mule deer country, but you'd be surprised at how many fly. Of course, whether you drive or not depends a lot on where you're coming from, and whether or not you'll be camping and hauling your own gear. Colorado, Wyoming and Montana, for instance, aren't horribly long drives from the Midwest, but heading to mule deer country from the East Coast or the South is another story.

Driving

No matter where you're coming from, give yourself ample drive time so you're not exhausted before it's even time to start hunting. The drive through some of America's widest and most open spaces is spectacular and coming to a higher altitude will take a toll on you no matter what physical shape you're in.

Flying

Flying is a good option, too, especially if you're going on a guided hunt or renting a vehicle and basing from a motel. You may even be able to pack enough gear to camp, especially if you're going light and packing in. You'd be surprised at how close you can get to good mule deer country, flying into places like Denver, Salt Lake City, Albuquerque, Boise, Cheyenne, Billings, Missoula, Pocatello and others.

Airlines today have strict regulations on shipping firearms. Here are several general rules to keep in mind. You'll want to ask the airline customer service department for details directly, to make sure you're up-to-date on the rules in today's changing world.

Firearms must be unloaded and enclosed within a locked, hard-sided case. An option is to have the firearm in the manufacturer's box, which must be enclosed in a soft-sided case, like a duffel bag, or hard-sided luggage that is locked. Be aware that the ticket agent, under current rules, will ask you to open up the case, right there in a crowded airport, and have you insert a tag you have signed indicating the firearm is unloaded. But having the tag inside is probably better than having it hanging outside, calling attention to the fact that your valuable firearm is inside.

Take along a roll of duct tape, and use it to tape that case shut real good, after you lock it back up. Wrap tape around the entire case, in several places. This is an extra safeguard against the case popping open and your rifle tumbling out onto the tarmac.

It's a good idea to store ammunition separately, for safety's sake, but no rule says you can't keep it in the case with the gun. Once again, ammunition must be checked luggage. You can't take it on board.

The rules for bows and arrows aren't quite as stringent, but you'll surely want to have a locked hard-sided case, and tape it shut as well. Arrows will ride well within that case, in the compartment made for them.

Hunting knives, broadheads, steel sharpening tools, pocket knives: go ahead and check them all. It's a good idea to carry your day pack with your binoculars, spotting scope, camera and other delicate, high-value items on board with you. Make sure you purge anything like the sharp steel items mentioned and store them in your checked luggage. Film up to 1000 ASA is safe going through the security scanners.

Most airlines will allow three checked pieces of luggage. A good combo is your rifle or bow case, a large duffel with your gear (clothes, etc.), and a cooler. Be aware, airlines will charge you,

probably up to $50, for extra checked bags, or for checked baggage over 70 pounds.

The meat from a boned-out and butchered mule deer buck will fit nicely in a good-sized cooler and, if cooled or frozen, should keep perfectly on your trip home. Take out any dry ice before checking the box or cooler, as dry ice is not allowed on the plane.

Once You Get There

Shoot your weapon once you reach camp. This is imperative for any hunter traveling to mule deer country. We repeat, SHOOT YOUR WEAPON AND MAKE SURE YOU'RE ON-TARGET, ONCE YOU GET TO YOUR DESTINATION.

The altitude and the bumps and jiggling of traveling can knock your finely-tuned rifle or bow out of kilter. It pays every time to shoot the arm before you hunt. If you need to adjust, you avoided some misses and problems. If the weapon is right-on, hunt with confidence!

BEING THERE

Being there in mule deer country is what it's all about. It is the reward for all your planning and hard work and provides you with the opportunity to harvest one of North America's greatest big game animals. The balance of this book covered many details on understanding mule deer, locating likely haunts, actually spotting the deer and then hunting to within range.

But one more idea is worth mentioning here. That is the attitude you'll need to hunt mule deer. Muley country can be a soft, warm, pleasant, "Indian Summer" type of place that will make you think you've found heaven on earth. It can also turn on you and deliver mean, wet, nasty conditions from rain to snow to pea-soup mist. Did we mention the winds that will blow for days and wear out your lungs and your eyes? No matter what the weather, most mule

deer country offers plenty of rocks, brush, steep slopes and other challenges of terrain that make the land starkly beautiful and tough to navigate effectively.

All this can get the better of you if you're not prepared through both your planning, and your attitude. Through it all, remember that over the next rise could be the buck of your dreams.

He may be bedded right out on the side of the canyon you're glassing, but it's up to you to find him. He may be feeding his way around the edge of those quakies over there, soon to be in your sights as you watch this feeding area for the evening. Drag yourself out of that warm sleeping bag on this, the fifth morning of your hunt, because a weather front is coming in and every buck on the mountain will be feeding into the daylight today. Don't sit at camp this afternoon and wonder where the deer are. They're somewhere out there in the rocks or sage or timber. Find a high spot and glass the countryside and its sheltered, shady spots until you find a buck. Instead of lamenting that you haven't had a "shooter" buck in your sights yet, realize that every hour you hunt you're that much closer to him.

These are the types of attitudes that will make you a successful, or a more successful, mule deer hunter. From river breaks to rolling prairie to piñon-juniper foothills to classic timbered mountains, mule deer country is vast and the only way you're going to get a buck fair-and-square is to get *out there* and do it.

You have to keep hunting – hard. And you have to keep your faith up and your effort high. The deer are there.

Remember, in a matter of mere seconds you can, and will, go from wondering how you're going to explain you didn't get a buck, to thinking this is one of the best hunts ever as you scramble your way down to the four-by-four you shot. Then again, you may have just picked up the blood trail of the wide-racked old patriarch who you know is lying somewhere ahead because your arrow passed completely through his chest as he stood up from his last bed. That's the nature of mule deer hunting. That's why you decided to experience it for yourself.

Good planning and the right attitude — such as spending every minute you can in the field, right up to the end of shooting light — will result in bucks like this.

Chapter 13

In Conclusion

It only takes about one trip to muley country to have trophy mule deer hunting enter your system and never let you rest. Big monster bucks who slip away are awesome spectacles as they top out over the skyline. They imprint an image on your mind that will keep you dreaming and scheming until you find yourself back in their magical hideouts, stalking the gray ghosts of peaks and prairies once again.

This book will help you be more successful in finding what you're looking for in mule deer country. True, we have presented a lot of information, and it will take time and experience to remember it all. So why not keep the book by your easy chair or couch, and brush up on your knowledge as you entertain dreams of gray-coated, wide-antlered bucks by a crackling fire? Browse these pages often during the summer, as you prepare for another autumn of hunting. Then take the book to camp, if you have the room. Use it to refresh your memory the evening before opening day; this will be a great way to adjust your mindset to mule deer hunting.

Every page of this book offers images and insights that will make you an even better mule deer hunter, or lead you to success with your first muley buck. We urge you to read every page, and refer to them often. But we also know that life is busy for everyone these days, so if you commit anything to your absolute memory, make it these three tactics:

Looking for Pieces and Parts

Skirting

Scrolling

These are the bases of good mule deer hunting. The rest will come with time, effort, and maybe a few cuss words. But you can and will eventually become a top-notch mule deer hunter. Good Luck!

One of the best ways to preserve our hunting heritage is to get young people involved in the sport.

And don't teach hunting to only the boys!

A Natural High

By Jim Van Norman

In closing, the following is a story I wrote as a young man, regarding the day I realized I had truly become a mule deer addict. I relate this story so you may prepare yourself for what lies ahead as you get sucked headlong into the world of trophy mule deer.

As the darkness fades and the landscape slowly comes into focus, my eyes scan and dance, hoping to see "them" before "they" discover me. A cool breeze bites at my nose, causing my eyes to water as I peer ever so slightly over the rocky edge. I pause momentarily, making certain my vision clears before proceeding on my stomach.

They have been seen here before, lying motionless, having made their rounds in the darkness and then bedding down to scan this domain from the prone position.

Creeping forward slightly, I peer into the rimmed washout – studying each rock, bush and blade of grass thoroughly. The shadows recede, as if slithering away, with the sun's emergence. Expectation suddenly doubles gravity, and I begin to feel a presence. I strain to detect an image. Abruptly my gaze is frozen, while right before me, scant yards away, they materialize.

Hidden in the shadows, but beginning to take form and emerge, are webs of branched sabers, polished to a glistening hue. The creature assigned to guard such creations, and who is equally magnificent in perfection, lies beneath. I try not to look directly into his eyes, as surely he'll feel my presence, but I'm drawn to stare in awe. Each saber extends upward toward infinity, like the long, crooked fingers of a wicked witch, reaching for a spell from thin air. I'm stunned, my body rivets to the ground.

The sun now unveils the entirety of each saber. They're incredible. Each is separate and piercing. Yet when moved, they all move regimentally, in synchronized motion, as if on some magical axis. As the adrenaline surges and almost overcomes me, the puff of a slight breeze on the back of my neck snaps me out of it. I grimace humbly to myself ... as the "keeper" with his "sabers of splendor" tests the air and vanishes.

I won't admit it to myself, but I'm relieved. For I'm not sure my nerves could have stood another second in the magnetic force field surrounding those phantom antlers and that big buck mule deer.

Now, I'm sure you thought the creatures from some black lagoon were about to emerge from the shadows and ring my neck. Not quite! But the suspense, I'm sure, couldn't have been any more mesmerizing. Sure, as a hunter, I'm a little disappointed that I didn't get the buck, but what a magnificent "in-your-face" spectacle for an outdoor adrenaline addict and thrill-seeker. I thank a power greater than us all for this opportunity.

I've hunted these wondrous critters since I was eleven years old and have yet to figure out completely what is so mystifying about the "keeper" and those "sabers." I often try to analyze what triggers the uncontrollable fever, that "adrenaline drunk" and "frozen brain" syndrome, that we all experience to some degree while hunting trophy mule deer. "Trophy" meaning any instigator of that adrenaline rush!

Does our subconscious override consciousness when they explode from underfoot or mysteriously materialize where there was nothing a glance ago? Is it the shape of the antlers that pulls a trigger of excitement and awe in the back of our minds? Do they resemble images we've cautioned our subconscious to beware of? Are they swords or blades, polished to perfection? Weapons for some sinister purpose? Or is it the antlers' finger-like, grasping appearance – like that of a wicked someone or ghostly something emerging from the shadows – that triggers a fear?

Does the shape bring us imagery – of a spider, upside-down in mid air, with its witchly and crooked appendages reaching in chilling synchronization? Is it that which startles the mind and widens the eyes?

Or, it could be the antlers' fire-like appearance, those tines of fire dancing before us with different lengths and varying widths, each tine a sharp, well-proportioned point of flame darting upward then disappearing, that stirs the coals of our soul. Fire, so soothing and warm yet deceptive.

Possibly, antlers are curved and cupped toward the heavens, gathering strength, magic and beauty directly from them. A deep subject for even the most focused thinkers.

And last, but certainly not least, there's the "keeper of the sabers" himself. The enchanted being we never grow tired of encountering/and the magical images portrayed in each of our minds as he transforms from the shadows where nothing existed an eyelash before. We worship his beauty and nobility; his coloration and definition; the amazing senses and extraordinary abilities displayed while guarding the sabers he so proudly carries to safety. This noble guardian is a natural magician, cued by some mystic telepathy and poised to detect any presence. And upon little cue, with one unanimous flow, the wizard will vanish. A truly sacred being, deserving of a startled poise.

So what shocks us into a mental state of limbo? What beckons us year after year to the haunts and magical hideouts of these ghostly beings? It is adrenaline, fear, hope, the unexpected, the unexplainable and the images hidden within. All brought to the forefront by the keeper and the sabers of splendor!

See what can happen? If it happens to you, for God's sake don't tell anyone, they'll think you're nuts! Not to worry though, they're gonna let me out this fall before opening day because I've shown improved rational imaging and good behavior.

Good luck in all your trophy mule deer quests! And best wishes, from both Tom and me, for many successful seasons!

JVN

Appendix

Other Mule Deer Reading

You're holding the best book available on mule deer hunting. But if you're interested in discovering even more details about the fascinating mule deer and its origins, history, habitat, habits and lifestyle, then here are some other great books:

Mule Deer Country. By Valerius Geist and Michael H. Francis. NorthWord Press.

Mule Deer: Behavior, Ecology, Conservation. By Erwin and Peggy Bauer. Voyageur Press.

The Deer of North America. By Leonard Lee Rue III. Lyons Press.

Mule and Black-tailed Deer of North America. Compiled and edited by Olaf C. Wallmo. The Wildlife Management Institute.

Big Game of North America. Various Authors. A Wildlife Management Institute Book.

Organizations

There are some great organizations you can join to help the mule deer and its habitat. As part of your membership you'll have the chance to meet people with similar interests and learn much through the publications these foundations publish.

Mule Deer Foundation
1005 Terminal Way, Suite 140
Reno, NV 89502
888-375-3337
702-322-2800

North American Pronghorn Foundation*
1905 CY Ave.
Casper, Wyoming 82604
307-235-NAPF

Rocky Mountain Elk Foundation*
P.O. Box 8249
Missoula, MT 59807-8249
406-523-4575

*Note that the latter two organizations, though not directly tied to mule deer, are concerned with habitat preservation of other wonderful Western species, and almost everything these groups do will also benefit muleys.

Trophy Scoring Sheets

Any mule deer, taken under the rules of fair chase in the wide-open spaces of the West, is a true hunting trophy. And a mature buck with his sweeping, double-forked antlers, will make your heart beat faster every time you think about the day you took him and the country you were in. As humans though, we like to put numbers with almost everything, and mule deer antlers are no exception. So if you've got a really big buck and want to see how he stacks up against the rest, here are scoring sheets from The Boone and Crockett Club (mule deer taken by all means). Pope and Young (archery only) uses the same scoring system. Addresses and phone numbers for these organizations are as follows:

Boone and Crockett Club
250 Station Dr.
Missoula, MT 59801
406-542-1888

Pope and Young Club
P.O. Box 548
Chatfield, MN 55923
507-867-4144

Score sheets reprinted with the permission of the Boone and Crockett Club.

OFFICIAL SCORING SYSTEM FOR NORTH AMERICAN BIG GAME TROPHIES

Records of North American
Big Game

BOONE AND CROCKETT CLUB®

250 Station Drive
Missoula, MT 59801
(406) 542-1888

TYPICAL
MULE DEER AND BLACKTAIL DEER

Kind of Deer: _____

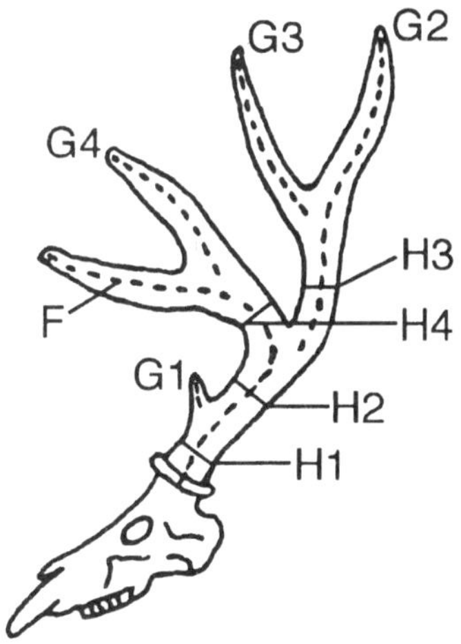

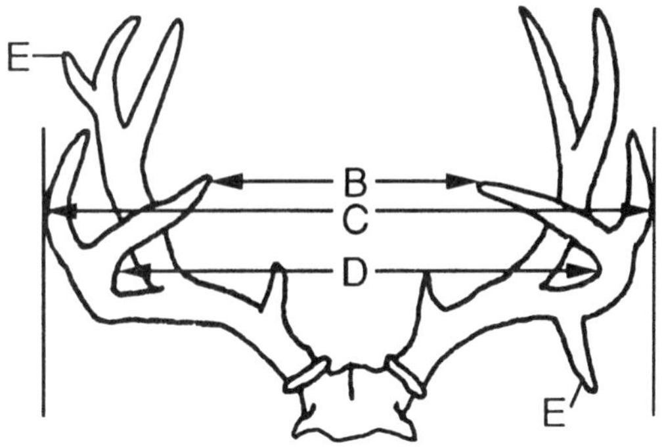

Minimum Score:	Awards	All-time
mule	180	190
Columbia	125	135
Sitka	100	108

Detail of Point Measurement

Abnormal Points	
Right Antler	Left Antler
Subtotals	
Total to E	

SEE OTHER SIDE FOR INSTRUCTIONS				Column 1	Column 2	Column 3	Column 4
A. No. Points on Right Antler		No. Points on Left Antler		Spread Credit	Right Antler	Left Antler	Difference
B. Tip to Tip Spread		C. Greatest Spread					
D. Inside Spread of Main Beams		(Credit May Equal But Not Exceed Longer Antler)					
E. Total of Lengths of Abnormal Points							
F. Length of Main Beam							
G-1. Length of First Point, If Present							
G-2. Length of Second Point							
G-3. Length of Third Point, If Present							
G-4. Length of Fourth Point, If Present							
H-1. Circumference at Smallest Place Between Burr and First Point							
H-2. Circumference at Smallest Place Between First and Second Points							
H-3. Circumference at Smallest Place Between Main Beam and Third Point							
H-4. Circumference at Smallest Place Between Second and Fourth Points							
			TOTALS				

ADD	Column 1		Exact Locality Where Killed:
	Column 2		Date Killed: Hunter:
	Column 3		Owner: Telephone #:
	Subtotal		Owner's Address:
SUBTRACT Column 4			Guide's Name and Address:
	FINAL SCORE		Remarks: (Mention Any Abnormalities or Unique Qualities)

I certify that I have measured this trophy on _____ 19 _____

at (address) _____ City _____ State _____

and that these measurements and data are, to the best of my knowledge and belief, made in accordance with the instructions given.

Witness: _____ Signature: _____

B&C Official Measurer [ ][ ][ ]

I.D. Number

INSTRUCTIONS FOR MEASURING TYPICAL MULE AND BLACKTAIL DEER

All measurements must be made with a 1/4-inch wide flexible steel tape to the nearest one-eighth of an inch. (Note: A flexible steel cable can be used to measure points and main beams only.) Enter fractional figures in eighths, without reduction. Official measurements cannot be taken until the antlers have air dried for at least 60 days after the animal was killed.

A. Number of Points on Each Antler: To be counted a point, the projection must be at least one inch long, with length exceeding width at one inch or more of length. All points are measured from tip of point to nearest edge of beam. Beam tip is counted as a point but not measured as a point.

B. Tip to Tip Spread is measured between tips of main beams.

C. Greatest Spread is measured between perpendiculars at a right angle to the center line of the skull at widest part, whether across main beams or points.

D. Inside Spread of Main Beams is measured at a right angle to the center line of the skull at widest point between main beams. Enter this measurement again as the Spread Credit **if** it is less than or equal to the length of the longer antler; if greater, enter longer antler length for Spread Credit.

E. Total of Lengths of all Abnormal Points: Abnormal Points are those non-typical in location such as points originating from a point (exception: G-3 originates from G-2 in perfectly normal fashion) or from bottom or sides of main beam, or any points beyond the normal pattern of five (including beam tip) per antler. Measure each abnormal point in usual manner and enter in appropriate blanks.

F. Length of Main Beam is measured from the center of the lowest outside edge of burr over the outer side to the most distant point of the Main Beam. The point of beginning is that point on the burr where the center line along the outer side of the beam intersects the burr, then following generally the line of the illustration.

G-1-2-3-4. Length of Normal Points: Normal points are the brow tines and the upper and lower forks as shown in the illustration. They are measured from nearest edge of main beam over outer curve to tip. Lay the tape along the outer curve of the beam so that the top edge of the tape coincides with the top edge of the beam on both sides of point to determine the baseline for point measurement. Record point lengths in appropriate blanks.

H-1-2-3-4. Circumferences are taken as detailed for each measurement. If brow point is missing, take H-1 and H-2 at smallest place between burr and G-2. If G-3 is missing, take H-3 halfway between the base and tip of G-2. If G-4 is missing, take H-4 halfway between G-2 and tip of main beam.

FAIR CHASE STATEMENT FOR ALL HUNTER-TAKEN TROPHIES

FAIR CHASE, as defined by the Boone and Crockett Club®, is the ethical, sportsmanlike and lawful pursuit and taking of any free-ranging wild game animal in a manner that does not give the hunter an improper or unfair advantage over such game animals.

Use of any of the following methods in the taking of game shall be deemed **UNFAIR CHASE** and unsportsmanlike:

I. Spotting or herding game from the air, followed by landing in its vicinity for the purpose of pursuit and shooting;

II. Herding, pursuing, or shooting game from any motorboat or motor vehicle;

III. Use of electronic devices for attracting, locating, or observing game, or for guiding the hunter to such game;

IV. Hunting game confined by artificial barriers, including escape-proof fenced enclosures, or hunting game transplanted for the purpose of commercial shooting;

V. Taking of game in a manner not in full compliance with the game laws or regulations of the federal government or of any state, province, territory, or tribal council on reservations or tribal lands;

VI. Or as may otherwise be deemed unfair or unsportsmanlike by the Executive Committee of the Boone and Crockett Club.

I certify that the trophy scored on this chart was taken in **FAIR CHASE** as defined above by the Boone and Crockett Club. In signing this statement, I understand that if the information provided on this entry is found to be misrepresented or fraudulent in any respect, it will not be accepted into the Awards Program and all of my prior entries are subject to deletion from future editions of *Records of North American Big Game* and future entries may not be accepted.

Date: _____ Signature of Hunter:_____
(Signature must be witnessed by an Official Measurer or a Notary Public.)

Date: _____ Signature of Notary or Official Measurer:_____

OFFICIAL SCORING SYSTEM FOR NORTH AMERICAN BIG GAME TROPHIES

Records of North American
Big Game

BOONE AND CROCKETT CLUB®

250 Station Drive
Missoula, MT 59801
(406) 542-1888

Minimum Score: Awards All-time
215   230

NON-TYPICAL
MULE DEER

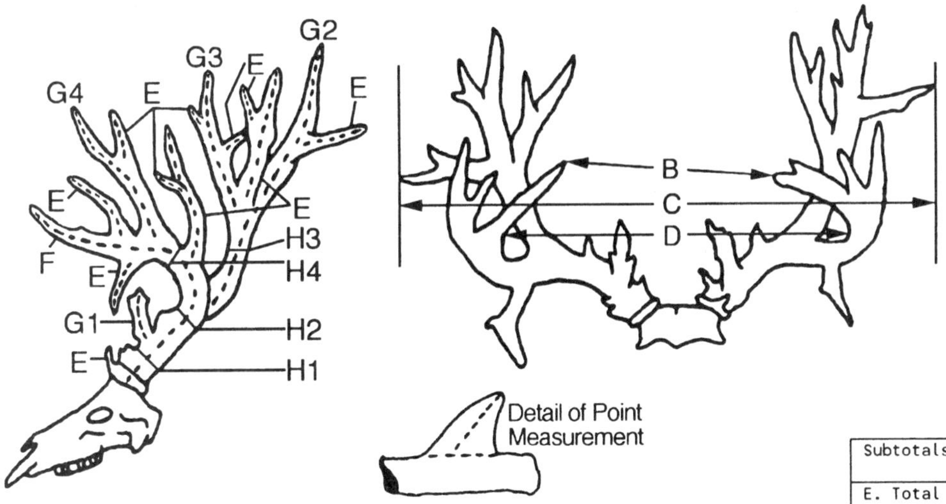

Detail of Point
Measurement

Abnormal Points	
Right Antler	Left Antler
Subtotals	
E. Total	

SEE OTHER SIDE FOR INSTRUCTIONS				Column 1	Column 2	Column 3	Column 4
A. No. Points on Right Antler		No. Points on Left Antler		Spread Credit	Right Antler	Left Antler	Difference
B. Tip to Tip Spread		C. Greatest Spread					
D. Inside Spread of Main Beams		(Credit May Equal But Not Exceed Longer Antler)					
F. Length of Main Beam							
G-1. Length of First Point, If Present							
G-2. Length of Second Point							
G-3. Length of Third Point, If Present							
G-4. Length of Fourth Point, If Present							
H-1. Circumference at Smallest Place Between Burr and First Point							
H-2. Circumference at Smallest Place Between First and Second Points							
H-3. Circumference at Smallest Place Between Main Beam and Third Point							
H-4. Circumference at Smallest Place Between Second and Fourth Points							
			TOTALS				

ADD	Column 1		Exact Locality Where Killed:	
	Column 2		Date Killed: Hunter:	
	Column 3		Owner: Telephone #:	
Subtotal			Owner's Address:	
SUBTRACT Column 4			Guide's Name and Address:	
Subtotal			Remarks: (Mention Any Abnormalities or Unique Qualities)	
ADD Line E Total				
FINAL SCORE				

I certify that I have measured this trophy on _____ 19 _____

at (address) _____ City _____ State _____

and that these measurements and data are, to the best of my knowledge and belief, made in accordance with the instructions given.

Witness: _____ Signature: _____

B&C Official Measurer ☐☐☐☐

I.D. Number

INSTRUCTIONS FOR MEASURING NON-TYPICAL MULE DEER

All measurements must be made with a 1/4-inch wide flexible steel tape to the nearest one-eighth of an inch. (Note: A flexible steel cable can be used to measure points and main beams only.) Enter fractional figures in eighths, without reduction. Official measurements cannot be taken until the antlers have air dried for at least 60 days after the animal was killed.

A. Number of Points on Each Antler: To be counted a point, the projection must be at least one inch long, with length exceeding width at one inch or more of length. All points are measured from tip of point to nearest edge of beam as illustrated. Beam tip is counted as a point but not measured as a point.

B. Tip to Tip Spread is measured between tips of main beams.

C. Greatest Spread is measured between perpendiculars at a right angle to the center line of the skull at widest part, whether across main beams or points.

D. Inside Spread of Main Beams is measured at a right angle to the center line of the skull at widest point between main beams. Enter this measurement again as the Spread Credit if it is less than or equal to the length of the longer antler; if greater, enter longer antler length for Spread Credit.

E. Total of Lengths of all Abnormal Points: Abnormal Points are those non-typical in location such as points originating from a point (exception: G-3 originates from G-2 in perfectly normal fashion) or from bottom or sides of main beam, or any points beyond the normal pattern of five (including beam tip) per antler. Measure each abnormal point in usual manner and enter in appropriate blanks.

F. Length of Main Beam is measured from the center of the lowest outside edge of burr over the outer side to the most distant point of the main beam. The point of beginning is that point on the burr where the center line along the outer side of the beam intersects the burr, then following generally the line of the illustration.

G-1-2-3-4. Length of Normal Points: Normal points are the brow tines and the upper and lower forks as shown in the illustration. They are measured from nearest edge of main beam over outer curve to tip. Lay the tape along the outer curve of the beam so that the top edge of the tape coincides with the top edge of the beam on both sides of point to determine the baseline for point measurement. Record point lengths in appropriate blanks.

H-1-2-3-4. Circumferences are taken as detailed for each measurement. If brow point is missing, take H-1 and H-2 at smallest place between burr and G-2. If G-3 is missing, take H-3 halfway between the base and tip of G-2. If G-4 is missing, take H-4 halfway between G-2 and tip of main beam.

FAIR CHASE STATEMENT FOR ALL HUNTER-TAKEN TROPHIES

FAIR CHASE, as defined by the Boone and Crockett Club®, is the ethical, sportsmanlike and lawful pursuit and taking of any free-ranging wild game animal in a manner that does not give the hunter an improper or unfair advantage over such game animals.

Use of any of the following methods in the taking of game shall be deemed **UNFAIR CHASE** and unsportsmanlike:

   I.   Spotting or herding game from the air, followed by landing in its vicinity for the purpose of pursuit and shooting;

   II. Herding, pursuing, or shooting game from any motorboat or motor vehicle;

   III. Use of electronic devices for attracting, locating, or observing game, or for guiding the hunter to such game;

   IV. Hunting game confined by artificial barriers, including escape-proof fenced enclosures, or hunting game transplanted for the purpose of commercial shooting;

   V.   Taking of game in a manner not in full compliance with the game laws or regulations of the federal government or of any state, province, territory, or tribal council on reservations or tribal lands;

   VI. Or as may otherwise be deemed unfair or unsportsmanlike by the Executive Committee of the Boone and Crockett Club.

I certify that the trophy scored on this chart was taken in **FAIR CHASE** as defined above by the Boone and Crockett Club. In signing this statement, I understand that if the information provided on this entry is found to be misrepresented or fraudulent in any respect, it will not be accepted into the Awards Program and all of my prior entries are subject to deletion from future editions of *Records of North American Big Game* and future entries may not be accepted.

Date: _____ Signature of Hunter: _____

(Signature must be witnessed by an Official Measurer or a Notary Public.)

Date: _____ Signature of Notary or Official Measurer: _____